Welcome to My Life

**A Personal Parenting
Journey Through Autism**

2nd Edition

Praise for
Welcome to My Life

"With exquisite detail and consummate honesty, Laurie Hellmann shares with us the unremitting challenges and ultimate rewards of raising her son with severe autism. You will live this alongside Laurie and her family and will understand her exhaustion, her frustration and her deep abiding love."

Emily Perl Kingsley
Parent, Advocate, Former *Sesame Street* Writer (45 Years) and Former Board Member for the National Down Syndrome Congress

"Laurie Hellmann's book about parenting with an autistic son is raw and wonderful. Her authenticity is palpable, and you feel her courage, love, and determination on every page. You will be inspired. Highly recommended!"

Cathy Fyock
Author, *The Speaker Author: Sell More Books and Book More Speeches*

"This is an amazing and emotional story about love, hope, faith and advocacy. Laurie pours her heart out in an attempt to tell her story and, in doing so, helps so many others. *Welcome to My Life* is a book you'll want to read more than once. It will be a blessing to so many!"

Kelly Davis
Autism Mom, @GrowingUpSteven

"I am a firm believer that special-needs children are a gift from God, sent to shape *us* into the people — parents, siblings, grandparents, friends, teachers, therapists, doctors, on-lookers — who *we* are supposed to be. Some people rise to the occasion and some people simply do not ... and those who do not rise will miss out on the transformative life lessons and life-changing blessings ripe for the taking. Laurie Hellmann minces no words in the telling of her raw and emotional story of her son's autism diagnosis and all that entails for their never-imagined new life. We watch her become a Warrior Mom as we read each line, and even though I know the special-needs journey in my own capacity, I feel the Warrior rise again in myself. With tears in my eyes, I can say thank you, Laurie, for keeping it real and raising awareness so the rest of us can have a deeper understanding of autism."

Rebecca Duvall Scott
Author of *Sensational Kids, Sensational Families: Hope for Sensory Processing Differences*, Speaker & Intervention Strategist

"An excellent book infused with faith and hope by an author who offers practical wisdom, humor, honesty, and grace. A MUST-READ for every parent and professional in the autism community. You'll experience autism from a new perspective of unconditional love and acceptance by Laurie's raw, honest, and humorous stories."

Ron Sandison
Author of *A Parent's Guide to Autism: Practical Advice. Biblical Wisdom.* and Founder of Spectrum Inclusion

"This book demonstrates the unconditional love of a mother toward her son, no matter the circumstances or personal cost. I have known Laurie throughout this journey and her unwavering advocacy for her 'Buddy' never ceases to amaze me."

Jeff Mathe, CRNA
Forever Friend

"Welcome to My Life will immediately take hold in your heart and connect you to the deep love of a mother for her son. Laurie Hellmann's honesty and raw emotion about her family and about her son's journey through autism offers us all lessons about acceptance, perseverance, courage, spirituality, strength and joy. Her story is proof that nothing is impossible, we should never give up and that, sometimes, it is in our deepest moments of despair where we find hope … hope in ourselves and hope in each other."

Penny Tate
Mental Health Specialist, Educator and Co-Author of *Manifesting Your Dreams: Inspiring Words of Encouragement, Strength and Perseverance*

"This book is a MUST-READ for anyone! You don't need personal experience with a loved one on the autism spectrum to feel the value of unconditional love from this memoir. Laurie's raw, honest and humorous journey will touch your heart … just as she's touched the lives of thousands of people like me."

Noopur Patel Ritter
Pharmaceutical Sales Director, Mom and Wife

"I love a book that rings true right from the get-go. As the mother of an adult son with autism, I know what real is, and Laurie nails it. Most of us struggle to just make it through the day, yet she somehow managed to pen this gloriously gut-wrenching, perfectly raw and honest book while still in the trenches. I can't imagine how. A true warrior mother, her determined fight for her son and her family is a magnificent read. I can't wait for the movie!"

Janet Pope, RN, BSN
Founding Member of Families for Effective Autism Treatment (FEAT) and Fellow Autism Warrior Mom

"I've been teaching at the middle school level for 25 years, and this book is an excellent resource for both teachers and students! Because we only see our students with special needs in a school setting, Laurie's book provides the context for a fuller understanding of the family supports, struggles and successes."

Beth Rayner
Educator, Creative Curriculum Advocate for Middle Schools, and Devoted Autism Aunt

"*Welcome to My Life* is an extremely powerful story of raising a child on the autism spectrum. As a fellow autism parent, I appreciate Laurie's honesty, advocacy and especially her humor. As we deal with the day-to-day, we need to laugh at the unknown and crazy that goes along with raising a child with a disability. This book is a definite must-read for anyone wanting to make our world a better, more inclusive place to live and thrive."

Malinda Dalton-Cook
Autism Parent and Co-Host of the Autism Mastermind Podcast

"Sometimes it's when you're on the brink of losing faith that you find exactly what you need most. Laurie Hellmann is a beautiful testament to how powerful the right perspective — and a little faith — can be in the midst of daily challenges. While no one's life is easy, Laurie faces unique obstacles daily while raising a special-needs child. But even in the thick of some of the hardest parenting struggles, Laurie finds blessings in each moment, seeing God ever-so-present throughout. Her book is a beautiful reminder that we all get the choice to find the silver linings — and to deepen our faith — every day."

Stephanie Feger
Author of *Color Today Pretty: An Inspirational Guide to Living a Life in Perspective* and Founder and Chief Strategist at emPower PR Group

"In her breathtaking debut book, Laurie L. Hellmann reminds us that 'If you've met one person with autism, you've met one person with autism.' And she's right ... every child or adult on the autism spectrum has a unique story and an individualized set of challenges and talents. I am married to a man on 'the other end' of the spectrum ... a man whose autism wasn't diagnosed until adulthood and whose specific diagnosis of Asperger's Syndrome puts him at a far remove from autistics like Laurie's son Skyler. But in many ways, the sensory processing issues, the rigid preferences for routine, and the general challenges of thinking and acting the way the neurotypical population expects them to is a universal daily and moment-to-moment challenge for every boy, girl, man or woman on the spectrum. Laurie's book does exactly what it promises — it welcomes us into her life to observe, to learn, to open our hearts and to become even stronger advocates for children and adults with special needs. As an Aspie wife, I found this book eye-opening and important. Whoever you are and whatever your vantage point, you're bound to agree."

Kate Colbert

Marketing Consultant and Coach, Aspie Wife and Author of *Think Like a Marketer: How a Shift in Mindset Can Change Everything for Your Business*

"*Welcome to My Life* is a heartwarming and at-times heart-wrenching memoir that beautifully illustrates the incredibly brave journey that autism parents and their autistic children take to advocate for inclusion and acceptance. Laurie's writing gives a voice to her extraordinary son's courage and achievements while navigating life with autism. This book is a must-read for any autistic person, parent, caregiver, teacher and professional who wants to become a strong advocate for autism inclusion."

Samantha Setty, MA, BCBA

Behavior Analyst and Director, Methodology: Excelling Through Behavior

"*Welcome to My Life* captures the vast struggles that face families raising a child with autism. Laurie Hellmann captures all these challenges with a sense of compassion and humor that only a mother of an autistic child can fully understand. This educational memoir will enlighten everyone who has the pleasure of reading it."

John Hackworth
Head Coach and Sporting Director for Louisville City FC, and Fellow Autism Parent

"Laurie Hellmann is a strong advocate who is leading the charge to help other families on their journey of raising a child with a diagnosis of autism. *Welcome to My Life: A Personal Parenting Journey Through Autism* is a real look at parenting, which is both honest and insightful. I appreciate this narrative, which is relatable as a fellow parent, author and advocate.

Teresa Unnerstall
DS-ASD Consultant and Author of *A New Course: A Mother's Journey Navigating Down Syndrome and Autism*

"In the era of posed and fabricated 'Insta-worthy' images of life, the vivid reality of our daily challenges is often hidden. For a special-needs parent, this is crippling. Isolation, self-doubt, and guilt often come hand-in-hand with the already-knee-buckling diagnosis of our precious child. In this book, Laurie Hellmann bravely and beautifully lifts the veil into the lives and struggles that so many of us endure alone, in silence. In doing so, she shares a remarkable story of inner strength and love for her family. *Welcome to My Life* should be required reading for *all* parents."

Jerry Turning (Mr. Bacon)
Blogger: "Bacon and Juice Boxes — Our Life with Autism"

"From the life-altering diagnosis to the small everyday wins, Laurie's unapologetically honest memoir will take you on an emotional journey as she navigates life with Skyler."

Emily Corum
Marketing Manager, Mother and Hellmann Family Friend

"*Welcome to My Life* is an educational memoir about the importance of inclusion, unconditional love and fierce advocacy to ensure all individuals with special needs are appreciated for their unique qualities and not demeaned for them."

Angie Abbott, PhD
Dietician, Assistant Dean of Health & Human Services at Purdue University, and Author's Lifelong Friend and Sorority Sister

"*Welcome to My Life* is an educational roadmap about the importance of unconditional love and fierce Mom advocacy. This book is a must-read for any families looking to navigate the complex world of inclusion for children with special needs."

Tom Harris
AVP for Business Development, Sage Care Therapy (Dallas TX)

"Laurie Hellmann's book offers deep insight into the life of bringing up a child on the autism spectrum. Autism is a 24/7 thing; it doesn't take a break. And while each autistic child is unique in their own way, they present enough similarities that we're all 'in this together.'"

Cliff Kresge
Autism Parent and Professional Golfer (PGA Tour Champions)

"*Welcome to My Life* is an educational memoir about a family's unconditional love and fierce advocacy for a child with autism, and demonstrates how these traits are, sadly, of absolute importance when navigating a medical system not yet fully aware of the special needs of these special children. I am honored to have met Skyler and his remarkable family. With this book, you will meet them too."

Arthur Krigsman, MD
Pediatric Gastroenterologist – Clinician, Researcher, Author

"*Welcome to My Life: A Personal Parenting Journey Through Autism* is a MUST READ! From the moment I turned the first page, I could feel the intense paradox of love and pain that a parent of an autistic child experiences. Although specifically about autism, this is truly a story of a mother's undying love for her son, period! So raw, so real and so beautiful! You don't have to have personal experience with autism to be inspired by this book."

Laura Leaton
Executive Coach, Trainer and Speaker, Anchored Elements Coaching and Training

Welcome to My Life

A Personal Parenting Journey Through Autism

2nd Edition

Laurie L. Hellmann

Endless Charades

Publishing

Welcome to My Life: A Personal Parenting Journey Through Autism

By Laurie L. Hellmann

Copyright 2020 by Laurie L. Hellmann;
Bonus Chapter Copyright 2024 by Laurie L. Hellmann

Published by Endless Charades Publishing (Aurora, CO).

First published in 2020 by Silver Tree Publishing
under its Silver Linings Media imprint.

Editing by:
Kate Colbert

Cover design and typesetting by:
Courtney Hudson Fox

Second edition, October 2024

ISBN: 979-8-9910758-3-1

Library of Congress Control Number: 2024920659

Created in the United States of America

Dedication

To Josh, for being the most supportive, loving and generous partner ... who finds humor in all things.

To Kendall, for being an amazing daughter and protector of your big brother.

And to Skyler, for your daily courage, determination and patience when teaching the world that there are alternate means of communication beyond speaking.

Table of Contents

.

CHAPTER ONE

My Sleep Number is Zero

I read somewhere recently that fatigue not only impacts a parent's health — in terms of their own cognitive functioning — but that it also impedes their ability to cope. Exhaustion can cause impaired functioning, forgetfulness, and reduced patience to such a degree that even normal activities can feel like overwhelming tasks. Add to that an extremely hyperactive, autistic teenager and that perfectly sums up the past 16 years of my life.

A typical weekend often equates to a 48-hour standoff between Skyler and our sanity.

A typical weekend often equates to a 48-hour standoff between Skyler and our sanity. For reasons unbeknownst to us, Skyler refuses to sleep on some nights and, instead, insists on clapping and banging on his bedroom walls all night long. When he's awake, we're awake

... no matter how hard we try. Despite turning off the baby monitor (which we use nightly to alert us if he wakes early or needs us), the loud banging noises echo through the house, making it impossible to sleep — unless you're our daughter, Kendall, whose room is across from Skyler's. She sleeps so soundly that a train could roll through the house and she wouldn't even know it! Color me envious.

During Skyler's solo slumber party, it's imperative for us to check on him every two hours to be sure he hasn't leaked urine through his "pull-up," or his extra diaper, waterproof briefs and/or pajama pants — a combination of protective clothing he must endure every night. The urine output this kid generates is impressive and was beyond all comprehension until his pediatric gastroenterologist reminded us recently that the steroid Skyler takes at night is likely to blame for the extreme fluid retention and release. (Sigh. Sometimes the "cure" is its own ailment.) Occasionally, during these all-nighters, Skyler will remain dry throughout most of the bed checks. But those are remarkable surprises and we generally know these "dry spells" won't last.

Bath-Time Before Sunrise

We are beyond exhausted and sleep deprived as we shuffle to his bedroom to conduct our fifth bed check at 3:45 a.m., so when we unlock the bottom Dutch-door of his custom made, built-in bed[1], Josh and I sigh deeply in unison upon finding that the dam had indeed broken, and that Skyler had peed through all protective layers ... as well as his bed sheets. *Damn it!* So, the hubby and I tag-team

---

1   When their house was originally designed, Skyler's bedroom was intended to have a walk-in closet but Laurie got the bright idea to make it larger and turn it into a fort-style bed for Skyler, who enjoyed cozy spaces. She padded the walls with thick foam covered by soft fleece fabric and had a custom queen mattress made that fits perfectly. She and Josh had the builder put a Dutch door on this special "bed room" with the top half of the door removed so Mom and Dad can see in and Sklyer can see out.

— one strips the bed while the other gives Skyler a quick bath and repackages his bottom half to get him back to bed as quickly and quietly as possible. As frustrating as this ordeal can be, we always do what needs to be done without hesitation or griping at each other (even though we're tired as hell and extremely irritable) because, after all, it is the reality that comes with a non-potty-trained child on the autism spectrum. And, certainly, is not Skyler's fault. We have learned that there's no point in being frustrated or angry when there's no one deserving of our negative emotions. We carry on. We sigh, we laugh, we roll our eyes. We do what we have to do.

We have learned that there's no point in being frustrated or angry when there's no one deserving of our negative emotions. We carry on. We sigh, we laugh, we roll our eyes. We do what we have to do.

Skyler finally gives in to the exhaustion around 5:45 a.m. and we try to get an hour or two of sleep, as well. However, the puppy has other plans. (Oh yes, because why wouldn't we want to use our vast knowledge of cleaning up accidents and complicate our lives with another "toddler?") The silver lining to frequently being awake at the crack of dawn, if I dig deep enough to find one, is that I rarely miss the most beautiful sunrises. We only let Skyler sleep until 11:00 a.m. because, if we let him hibernate any longer, the entire situation from the previous sleepless night will rear its ugly head again ... and thus a horrible nighttime routine begins, night after night. And there's only so much we can take.

Welcome to Our Weekends

Skyler's normal Saturday or Sunday begins with him grinning ear to ear as he zombie-walks down the stairs, headed directly to the kitchen table for breakfast. He eats the same thing every morning: Jimmy Dean sausage breakfast bowl, Activia yogurt and pulp-free orange juice. Josh or I scoot next to him on the bench at our kitchen table, always on his right side, and assist him with eating. We scoop up a spoonful of food and set the spoon on the plate or bowl for him to then independently lift to his mouth. Due to Skyler being non-verbal, the entire day consists of a series of questions posed to him, with the hope that he chooses exactly what he wants by pointing. Meals are no exception. So while he's eating, we'll say, "Skyler, do you want this or this?" ... pointing and defining the item in clearer detail. Skyler will then point to either his drink or the food item he wants and this continues until the food is gone or until he gets up from the table (usually leaving one or two bites behind), indicating he's finished.

Frequently, while still chewing, Skyler will get the sudden urge to leave his seat and make a lap or two around the kitchen — all while pulling semi-chewed food from his mouth, leaving a trail behind him (to the delight of the puppy) before returning to the table for another serving. Round and round and round we go.

Following breakfast, much of the day adheres to a very strict and exhausting schedule — pretty much like the movie *Groundhog Day*! It is imperative that we keep Skyler occupied and entertained, preferably out of the house; otherwise, he remains in perpetual motion, making laps around the kitchen and living room, wreaking havoc. His favorite ways to garner attention — while making us lose our patience and minds — are to bang on counters and walls or to repeatedly slam kitchen drawers open and closed, to grab and throw any item within reach from kitchen counters or tables, to hurl puppy toys in various directions, and to aggressively tug on curtains and unsus-pecting ponytails. Bottom line — *He. Doesn't. Sit. Down.* At least not until he's beyond exhausted and ready for bed. Skyler cannot be left unattended for even one minute, because the amount of destruction he's capable of creating during that brief period is remarkable. If, for some reason, Josh or I are flying solo for the day, we can forget about taking a shower or attending to much of anything on our to-do list.

> **Skyler cannot be left unattended for even one minute, because the amount of destruction he's capable of creating during that brief period is remarkable.**

To fill Skyler's need for attention and try to keep our sanity, we've identified some regular activities he reluctantly partici-pates in. During the spring and summer months, we will take an early-morning family walk through our neighborhood or visit a local park before the temperature gets prohibitively hot. Skyler doesn't enjoy walking and struggles keeping his hands to himself, so Josh most often pushes him in our amazing Kool-Stride jogging stroller, while Kendall and I tag along walking our boxer pup. When we return home, we instinctively glance at the clock and break into a pretty hardy laugh because, well, that only wasted about an hour of the day. *Now, what to do for the next seven hours until bedtime?* This time is usually filled with several of the 10+ *Sesame Street* DVDs we own (*Elmo's World* is the hands-down favorite) until the boss demands lunch. Any of us can quote the entire episode – of *every* episode and every topic Elmo has covered. I would estimate we've seen each one 400 times, at the very least.

The same process we employed for breakfast is then re-enacted for lunch. Luckily, Skyler is not a picky eater and he seems to enjoy most of the gluten-free meals I prepare for him. Most Saturdays, however, include a car ride to pick up his preferred weekend lunch — a burrito bowl from Qdoba. The road trip to the restaurant to pick up his food not only passes some time, but is truly one of the highlights of Skyler's day. Standing in line as they craft his perfect meal, exactly the same way each time — "chicken and rice, no beans, corn, queso, guac and cheese" (which is how we sing it to him on the drive to the tune of whatever hip hop song is on the radio) — elicits pure joy, evident by the huge smile on his face.[2]

Once lunch has been consumed, usually *inhaled*, and Skyler's belly is visibly full, he often attempts to sneak up to his room to take a nap or, if he's too tired to make it upstairs, he will plop down on the couch and start nodding off. If we allow the nap, it is only for an hour because anything longer will negatively affect his ability to sleep at night, and, well … you know how his sleepless nights turn out for us all! With or without a nap, we kick off the late afternoon with either a swim in the pool, if the weather permits, or we take another family walk.

So Many Hours Yet to Fill …

Although a quick swim in the pool sounds fantastic to most people, let me just explain that the process of getting Skyler ready for the swim is extensive. First, we have to reflect back on his bodily output for the day (i.e., has he pooped yet?) because if he hasn't, chances are strong that he will in the pool. We lather his upper body in

---

2   It should be noted that the Qdoba team at our local restaurant is amazing. We've had numerous chats with the Qdoba manager, where we've expressed our repeated thanks to him for all the extra kindness he and the staff have shown Skyler, on many occasions. They once gave him a "Team Qdoba" hat and T-shirt! We know they love and appreciate our heavy investment in their store. Not only do the employees have his order memorized, but witnessing Skyler's excitement over such a simple thing seems to give each of them a bigger smile, knowing they played a part in making his day special.

sunscreen, put on both his cloth swim diaper and swim trunks, take turns putting swimsuits and sunscreen on ourselves, and head outside. Our pool is called a Sports Bottom style because it has two shallow ends with a very small deep end sandwiched in the middle. Skyler's preference is to either pace wall to wall, stand in place, or — most often — he wants to be bounced up and down while sitting on one of our hips (which is damn near impossible for me to do with Skyler, since he's now taller than me!). The entire time we're in the pool, which is never more than 30 minutes and sometimes is just a few, we are continuously checking his britches for any sign of an accident about to happen. We've learned over time that his non-verbal indication of needing to get out and use the bathroom is to simply make his way to the steps and climb out. You might say to yourself, *"Well duh, that's obvious,"* but he used to always want to get out the minute he got in — with no poop involved in the equation — so we were clearly confused at this change of cue. Back before Skyler was more aware of what his body was telling him, we were always frantically jumping out of the "cesspool" to grab a skimmer and to dump massive amounts of chemicals into the pool to treat the water. Suffice it to say that it was a "shock" for us all! As Grover so eloquently sings in "Elmo's Potty Time," "Accidents happen, that's what they say. Accidents happen, they happen night or day." *Don't I know it, Grover!?*

If it's raining or wintertime — which puts us on a constant struggle-bus for outing ideas to eliminate cabin fever — we may walk the mall or just drive around with no particular destination in mind. On Saturday evenings, we usually attend 5:00 p.m. mass at our church and then take Skyler to his favorite restaurant or someplace with similar menu offerings — a bun-less cheeseburger with mashed potatoes for dinner. At the restaurant, it's clear to see that he loves the comfortable, padded booth seat and I think he equally enjoys the rapid attention he receives from the waiters and waitresses as he bangs on the table, demanding service like a medieval king!

We return home just in time for his bath, which lately takes every bit of patience I can muster (and often a fresh, dry T-shirt for me when it's done). These days, Skyler's 17-year-old, 125-lb. frame is the exact length of the tub, so he barely fits. He finds it beyond hilarious to splash around like a toddler, leaving me soaked to the bone and extremely annoyed. We've recently tried giving Skyler a shower, but that presents its own set of challenges. Both Josh and I have to participate, with one of us dressed in our swimsuit to assist with the showering and the other standing by with the towel to help get him out. It's a bigger hassle than getting splashed during the bath, so I figure I'll stick with the bathtub until it's no longer an option. Heck, maybe at that point we'll buy a new, handicap-accessible tub. As with every teenage boy, the inevitable signs of puberty, including facial hair, arrived a few years ago, which added another necessary grooming step for us to manage. Without hesitation, Josh voluntarily took on the task of shaving Skyler's face. Believe me — I was thrilled to remove myself from that chore, because I know absolutely nothing about beards or five o'clock shadows. Thankfully, Skyler doesn't mind the process and actually sits still while Josh carefully slides that straight razor down his cheek!

In addition to the bathing and shaving ritual, we must also lather Skyler's heels and palms of his hands in multiple ointments and creams, in an attempt to heal the massive cracking and splitting of his skin. Ever since he was three years old, he has had extreme skin issues that doctors struggle to diagnosis as anything other than eczema. The fissures in his heels are so gaping that they resemble a road in the aftermath of an earthquake.

Last up on the personal hygiene list is to assist Skyler, hand-over-hand, with brushing his teeth and putting on his teenage "smell goods" (deodorant) before exiting the bathroom and heading into the final phase of our long day.

Our evenings usually conclude with some couch sitting during "NBC Nightly News," "Wheel of Fortune," and — if he can make it without nodding off like a little old man — "Jeopardy." The minute Josh asks — in the form of a Jeopardy question of course, "The question on everyone's mind ..." to which I answer, "What is .. *Are you ready for bed, Buddy*?" — Skyler jumps up from the couch and insists on holding our hands while walking his groggy self up the stairs to his bedroom. The nightly triple-wrapping with the pull-up, diaper and waterproof briefs occurs again and the "I love yous," hugs and smooches are doled out. Josh and I head back downstairs to do a few, nearly silent small chores, all the while praying that Skyler will sleep through the night. Proud that we made it through another Saturday, often running on only a few hours of sleep to begin with, we finally get the chance to exhale deeply. Despite being completely exhausted and ready for bed ourselves, we shake it off and look forward to spending quality time with Kendall.

> **Proud that we made it through another Saturday, often running on only a few hours of sleep to begin with, we finally get the chance to exhale deeply.**

It's so nice that at 15 years old, Kendall still enjoys hanging out with us old people, watching movies and making homemade pizzas. I actually dread the day of putting Skyler to bed at 7:30 p.m. and at the same time, Kendall grabs the car keys and ditches us to meet up with her friends. The years fly by and regardless of feeling like I zombie-walk my way through life, I don't want to miss a single moment with either of my kids.

A final check of the baby monitor at 10:00 p.m. reveals the sounds of a snoring Skyler — thank goodness! So Josh and I jump into bed for what we hope will be at least five to six hours of sleep. After all, we need to rest and recuperate in order to have enough energy to repeat this entire day again tomorrow!

CHAPTER TWO

The Diagnosis

I think it's safe to say that most mothers don't forget the details of their child's birth. I remember them all. It's still a mystery why I went into labor five weeks early but, within a few hours of arriving at the hospital (during the last half of the Syracuse v. Kansas 2003 NCAA National Championship game, the outcome of which would decide my winning or losing the bracket pool with my friends) and just 20 minutes of pushing, my adorable little 6-pound boy, Skyler, arrived. Following delivery, I was transferred to my recovery room, where it seemed like hours ticked by before the nurse and on-call pediatrician arrived — without my newborn.

The physician spoke first. "I brought Nurse Kathy in with me because she was the one who initially bathed your son and was then tending to him in the nursery."

I just stared at him, not really registering his words while horrific scenarios rushed through my mind. Did the nurse drop Skyler?

Or drown him accidentally? What was the relevance of bringing up his bath?

The physician continued, "We have identified what we feel are minor issues with Skyler but are sending him for additional testing to know for sure. In addition, he tested positive for Beta Strep [a bacterial infection babies can catch from their mother during childbirth, which could cause complications like pneumonia, meningitis or sepsis if not treated effectively] and is currently receiving IV antibiotics, so he will need to remain in the Special Care Nursery for now."

Panicked and hormonal, I tried to comprehend every word but only picked up "minor issues," "IV" and "you can see him in a little while." Those few hours waiting, childless in my hospital recovery room, were agonizing. Not only were the nurses unable to bring him to me, but due to the epidural, which was still in full effect — rendering my legs useless, I had to wait for a wheelchair to arrive so I could be taken to the Special Care Nursery to even see him.

> **Those few hours waiting, childless in my hospital recovery room, were agonizing.**

At long last, I was given the green light to head down to the nursery to see my baby, but the nurse cautioned me that he would have several bandages on his tiny arms and legs because they struggled finding a proper vein for his IV. *Holy shit, people! This is not how I'd planned for my entrance into motherhood.* I bawled hysterically when I finally saw my beautiful little surfer boy, as the nurses called him, looking tan from jaundice with the thickest, curly, white-blond hair. Aside from being laid out in the phototherapy bed to reduce his bilirubin level, an IV line coming from his forehead and several monitor leads on his tiny chest, he looked completely normal. I was not able to hold him due to the cords, wires and the requirement that he remain in the phototherapy bed, so I parked my wheelchair close to him and remained next to his side with his hand wrapped around my finger until the nursing staff kicked me out. Little did I know that the first day of his life would be so symbolic — I have continued holding Skyler's hand to guide him and fight for answers every single day since.

The physician came to my hospital room later that evening and explained the reasoning behind all the specific tests he had ordered and the results of each one. He ordered a CT scan of Skyler's entire body because, while bathing him, the nurse noticed that Skyler had a condition called hypospadias (a birth defect in boys where the opening of the urethra is not located in the correct position), which often presents with part of the penis foreskin missing, looking like a partial circumcision. The CT also revealed that Skyler's kidneys were fused into the shape of a horseshoe and that Skyler had a small blood spot on his brain. While none of those abnormalities resulted in anything hugely significant for Skyler's overall health, what would follow — many weeks and months later — were severe developmental delays, affecting Skyler's fine and gross motor functions. Although I was traumatized with worry throughout the entire ordeal during his first few days of life, I am grateful the physician and nursing staff were so thorough.

At Home and at a Loss

I was completely set on nursing Skyler, and during our first few days home from the hospital, he cooperated nicely by latching on without much hesitation. However, throughout the entire feeding, he would cry hysterically and loudly. Frantic, I called my sister, who had experience nursing her children with great success and she gave me several ideas to try. Nothing seemed to work, and I feared the poor baby was starving because the feedings were so short, resulting in plenty of milk leftover to pump. I even tried giving him bottled breast milk, but he struggled to consume even a few ounces.

I eagerly attended my first scheduled pediatrician appointment when Skyler was a week old, hoping to get some help or answers, albeit fearful of being reprimanded. When taking Skyler's measurements, it was noted that he had lost almost a full pound and was now 5 pounds 2 ounces, only confirming my suspicion that he was definitely having issues with swallowing or sucking. The doctor appeared perturbed and threatened that if I didn't get some milk into Skyler, she would insist on placing a feeding tube! I felt attacked and judged, as if she believed I was purposely starving my newborn. This defensive moment marked the beginning of my future: advocating for my child and forcing the medical community to look deeper for explanations.

This was the beginning of my future: advocating for my child and forcing the medical community to look deeper for explanations.

I looked at the doctor with a "slow your roll, lady" glance and told her that I had hoped, instead of giving a new mother an ultimatum, she would provide some assistance or suggestions on how to get Skyler to properly eat and that she could help uncover the underlying issue causing my baby's malnourishment and weight loss. I explained that I understood how breastfeeding works and that the hospital nurses even identified how easily and correctly he latched on, but it appeared he was struggling to instinctively use his mouth muscles to suck. We agreed to halt attempts at nursing and to try bottle feeding exclusively.

At first, I pumped as often as possible to store up plenty of breast milk for him. When my ducts seemed to be running dry, I contacted the doctor's office for guidance and was instructed to drink a beer a day to help increase the milk production (which shocked the hell outta me, but I complied!). Any mom of a newborn deserves a beer, at the very least.

Skyler still wasn't consuming much, so I assumed it was an issue with the bottles. I quickly made my way to Target to purchase every style of bottle and nipple on the market, to hopefully correct the issue. No change. After a week, the daily beer was no longer effective and my milk ducts had completely dried up, so I frantically called the doctor's office again and was told to move on to formula, which presented additional challenges. I tried every brand available with the same result each time — Skyler was projectile vomiting after consuming approximately an ounce. I was then advised to try soy formula, given very slowly, half an ounce at a time, taking a break for 5-10 minutes between each "dose" formula; that seemed to finally work. Throughout this entire timeframe where he was practically starving, Skyler had the incredible ability to sleep soundly for at least five-hour stretches and required being woken to take a bottle. Thankfully, after several weeks, we made a positive turn and Skyler succeeded at gaining some weight and growing, although his measurements would never meet the applicable height and growth standards for his age.

The First Years – Quiet and Heart-Wrenching

Being a new mom and an avid reader, I had practically memorized all the most popular parenting books. I recall making some mental notes that Skyler didn't seem to be doing some of the things the experts said he should be doing. At the three-month mark, when most babies are smiling, lifting their heads during "tummy time" and starting to babble, Skyler continued sleeping the days away and was void of any of those early signs of activity. I tried not to worry much and kept reminding myself that he was technically a preemie, so no need for overreacting. The pediatrician did not demonstrate any signs of concern, and I suppose her dismissal, in a way, confirmed that I was probably just misreading the situation. Sadly, this would be the first time of many when I ignored my mother's intuition or gut feeling and replaced it with professional medical advice that I thought I could rely on.

> **At the three-month mark, when most babies are smiling, lifting their heads during "tummy time" and starting to babble, Skyler continued sleeping the days away and was void of any of those early signs of activity.**

At the seven-month mark, according to many sources and parents with children Skyler's age, Skyler should have been rolling over from tummy to back, sitting without help, raking objects closer and responding to his name when called. Now, I was overcome with panic. My precious little boy had not attempted any of those milestones and seemed completely disinterested in my face or his surroundings. The "information age" hadn't fully been born (with the internet and Google really just in their infancy at this time), so I lacked insights and connection that I desperately needed. I was stuck inside my own frightening thoughts until our next appointment with the pediatrician.

By this point, I was on edge and it showed during Skyler's eight-month checkup. The physician noted that Skyler was severely hypotonic (commonly known as "floppy baby syndrome"), which meant that he had very low muscle tone. When held, he hung in my arms like a rag doll. The doctor also agreed that Skyler wasn't hitting any of the developmental milestones he should be. She then informed me that he was "significantly developmentally delayed" and suggested we contact First Steps of Indiana — a state-funded therapy program for patients ages 0-3. I was in shock, but told myself I could tackle this minor setback. I believed it was, in fact, just a setback … not a permanent state of being.

From that point forward, our home became a revolving door of therapists; physical therapists, occupational therapists and speech therapists rotated in and out, multiple days a week. The improvements to Skyler's gross motor and fine motor skills were very slow to appear, but eventually he learned to sit up on his own and rake-grasp some of his food items to attempt to feed himself.

Skyler never crawled, but instead developed his own unique way of moving around. He would rest the top of his head on the floor with his legs behind him, his body in the shape of a tripod, and would shift his weight backward to move around. I could always tell where he was headed or what toy he was after because he would scan the room from a seated position then transition to his tripod stance, moving quickly toward the toy.

The walking came much later, at around three years old. For many months leading up to a more stable and confident gait, he carefully navigated around our house looking a bit like Frankenstein — slow and deliberate with each foot placement, legs wide apart and toes pointed out, his arms straight out in front of himself to keep his balance.

The one area of development that seemed to elude Skyler completely was verbalization; he couldn't or wouldn't mimic even a sound made by the speech therapist. He remained silent. During each quarterly and annual review with his case manager and respective therapists, we were repeatedly told that we shouldn't worry about the speech, with the rationale changing each meeting. We heard, "Skyler is working through so many other physical challenges with PT and

OT, so it's understandable that his brain is focusing elsewhere — his speech will come." And my personal favorite: "Boys tend to be slower to hit milestones; he'll speak when he's ready."

Soon after Skyler turned two years old, one of the therapists noted some concerns with his poor eye contact and non-responsiveness to his name being called. It was suggested that I have his hearing and vision tested, so of course I made an appointment right away. There were thorough examinations and nothing abnormal was noted, but shortly thereafter my world would take another dramatic and emotional turn.

I was finishing up our normal daily routine by giving Skyler a bath before putting him to bed. When I lifted him from the tub and began drying him off, his facial expression seemed frozen, his eyes focused forward, as if he was staring into space and completely absent. I attempted to startle him by loudly calling his name and noticed at that point his skin starting to take on a bluish tint. I instinctively started patting on his back and raking inside of his mouth to see if he was choking on an object but couldn't find anything. I screamed for his dad (my then husband) to call an ambulance and prayed to God that Skyler wasn't dying right before my eyes. By the time the ambulance arrived, Skyler's skin color had returned to normal, and he began looking around the room as if he was back from the brief coma he had been in. The entire random event seemed to last an eternity when, in actuality, it was only about two minutes. Skyler was exhausted and could barely keep his eyes open, so I declined taking the ambulance to the hospital. It was likely an idiotic thought but, at the time, I assumed this had been a freak, unique incident and there was likely nothing the hospital could do without knowing the cause. I assured the EMTs that I would follow up with his pediatrician the following day and when they left, I put Skyler to bed and laid on his floor next to his crib, watching his little body rise and fall with each breath the entire night.

The next day, during our office visit, the pediatrician asked a bunch of obvious questions like "Could he have swallowed any small pieces of a bath toy?" and "Did he eat or drink anything new that he may have been allergic to?" and "Was he acting strangely throughout the day?" I answered no to all of them. Considering his developmental delays and now this new random event, the doctor referred us to a local pediatric neurologist — the only one in town at the time. Due to Skyler's tender age (and after cashing in a few favors from my friends in the medical community), the neurology office was able to get us in rather quickly. I was grateful but their responsiveness actually sent me into a slight panic that we were dealing with something serious enough that the experts all agreed it needed to be addressed pronto.

During that first appointment, the neurologist was very thorough with his questioning and without much hesitation, he confidently explained that Skyler had actually experienced a seizure called Epileptic Aphasia. I was in shock and had a million questions — my little baby had a seizure? Why? Would he have more? How will I know if he's having one or preparing to have one? What can we do to stop the seizures or treat the condition? The neurologist first ordered an EEG (to analyze electrical activity in the brain) and wanted us to do some additional testing before starting any seizure medication.

Following the EEG, Skyler appeared to be fine and hadn't had another episode of zoning out or turning blue. So, I started thinking that maybe the bathtub incident was a freak event and he was inappropriately diagnosed with a seizure disorder. However, my relief wouldn't last long ... and the scariest event was yet to come.

On August 23, 2005, the weekend of my 30th birthday, my then-husband threw me a surprise birthday celebration and arranged that my mom surprise me by coming down to Indiana from Michigan. The following morning, we were chatting while she was holding Kendall, who was only three months old at the time, and I kept saying, "Skyler needs to wake up so he can see his Nana before she leaves." Knowing that Skyler was an incredible sleeper, I wasn't too alarmed that it was 9:30 a.m. and there were no noises coming from his baby monitor. However, he needed to eat and likely needed his diaper changed so I went upstairs to wake him.

What I saw and heard the moment I opened Skyler's bedroom door was one of the scariest moments of my life. The room was dark and still but, as I edged closer to his crib, I heard the horrifying sounds of Skyler gasping for air and gurgling on snot and phlegm. I frantically scooped up his completely limp and blue little body. I screamed at the top of my lungs "OH MY GOD! CALL AN AMBULANCE, HE'S SEIZING!!"

The ambulance quickly arrived, and paramedics attached an oxygen mask and several wires to Skyler before loading us both up — me on the gurney with my toddler's frail body in my lap. My fears turned to panic when the EMTs in the back of the ambulance shouted to the driver their code for "step on it," to which he immediately flipped on the lights and sirens and sped down the highway to the children's hospital emergency room. My husband frantically sped behind in his car, unaware of what was happening to our little boy.

We spent the next five hours in an exam room with a very lethargic and hungry two-year-old and weren't getting many answers. Being that I was actively nursing Kendall at that time, my body didn't bother to deviate from her feeding schedule just because Skyler needed me. My breasts were painfully engorged and I had to relieve the pressure. I practically cried as I squeezed out plentiful amounts of liquid gold, flushing it down the nearest toilet. I kept calling home to check on my mom and Kendall. I was equally worried that the minimal amount of pumped breast milk I had in our freezer would run out before we returned home and that Kendall would be starving and wailing uncontrollably. I felt like a horrible mother, unable to care for either of my babies in the precise way they each needed me.

I felt like a horrible mother, unable to care for either of my babies in the precise way they each needed me.

We were finally discharged from the hospital and instructed to follow up with our neurologist. We walked out without oxygen, monitors or any hope that this crisis wouldn't recur again in the coming hours. We were already scheduled to meet with neurology that week to undergo an MRI and begin his first seizure medication. Once all the brain monitoring was completed and we were a few weeks into the medication, we returned for the follow-up appointment. Unlike any prior appointment, the neurologist shifted gears a bit during this one and asked some questions regarding Skyler's development — specifically about his communication and cognition skills. I thought this conversation was odd, but I played along. It was at this point that the term Autism Spectrum Disorder (ASD) first entered my vocabulary. Autism. It was a lot to process.

The neurologist very nonchalantly began highlighting the various signs of autism and mentioned that, in his medical opinion, Skyler exhibited many clear signs of the disorder. He proceeded to share some information about "special programs" to look into, so we could "get the most out of him while he's still young." Finally, the physician presented a grim prognosis for the future by telling me Skyler would likely never walk, talk or function normally without the need for assistance.

I admittedly didn't handle the news well. Maybe it was the lackadaisical way the doctor delivered his opinion or his matter-of-fact determination that basically my two-year-old would be incapable of doing much beyond what he was already doing now, but it fired me up! I gathered what composure I could muster and said, "With all due respect to your clinical opinion, you've known Skyler all of five minutes and you're clairvoyant enough to foresee his entire future?!"

To say I was pissed is an understatement. I knew, that very day and that very moment, that I would do everything in my power to prove this physician — with his horrific bedside manner — wrong. I was bound and determined to fight for my son. Thus, a devoted Autism Warrior Mom and special-needs advocate was born.

> **I knew, that very day and that very moment, that I would do everything in my power to prove this physician — with his horrific bedside manner — wrong. I was bound and determined to fight for my son.**

I immediately contacted our pediatrician, who further explained that she would feel more comfortable assigning the "temporary" diagnosis of PDD-NOS (Pervasive Developmental Disorder — Not Otherwise Specified) as it relates to the diagnosis of autism, and she suggested we contact the Christian Sarkine Autism Treatment Center for a more detailed evaluation and official diagnosis. The Sarkine Center is housed within Riley Children's Hospital in Indianapolis, Indiana, and is part of Indiana University School of Medicine. I knew very little about autism and I didn't know whether to feel hope or despair. Being that this was 2005, autism was not discussed as openly as it is now and messages of hope were nowhere to be found. So, to be blatantly told that my two-year-old had essentially no chance at a normal life was, for me, beyond devastating and overwhelming. I had no contexts for this news — no friends who had been through it before, no experience with other children with autism, no knowledge bank of information I'd read or seen in the news.

I contacted the Autism Center and was informed that the waiting list to be evaluated by one of the specialists was approximately a year and a half! I was devastated, and I had them put Skyler on the waiting list. That year of waiting was the longest year of my life up to this point, but I didn't waste a single day sitting around twiddling my thumbs. At this time, Facebook was just a new fad for college students, Twitter and Instagram hadn't been invented, and Google was still somewhat foreign to me (meaning I wasn't that far removed from dial-up internet). As such, I had to rely on my old-school research skills. I dove head-first into any medical journals and magazine articles that merely mentioned autism, and I fired off tons of questions to all of Skyler's therapists. I practically begged to be connected to any and all families who had a child on the autism spectrum, so they could help prepare me for what could be in store. In case the autism diagnosis was accurate, I wanted to be one step ahead and constantly in the know.

> **I practically begged to be connected to any and all families who had a child on the autism spectrum, so they could help prepare me for what could be in store. In case the autism diagnosis was accurate, I wanted to be one step ahead and constantly in the know.**

While waiting for Skyler's official autism diagnosis, I kept hitting roadblocks. I was trying to maintain therapy sessions to ensure Skyler wouldn't suffer regression with his growth and progress thus far. After a lot of hard work, he began walking at around 36 months, learned to carefully navigate (on his knees) up and down stairs, and was able to feed himself independently with finger food. At this time in our lives, I was juggling the all-consuming responsibilities of caring for Skyler and Kendall while trying to come to terms with the difficult dynamics of a marriage in crisis. I was also working full-time in pharmaceutical sales, and the love and "normalcy" of my future life with Josh — who I would meet three years after separating from Skyler and Kendall's dad — was far from my mind and beyond my dreams. I was just trying to figure out what to do with the next hour of my life ... how to keep my kids happy and safe and healthy. It was a daily struggle.

Finally, a Diagnosis

Sadly, the First Steps program, through which we obtained all our therapists and support, concluded on Skyler's 3rd birthday, and he was then registered to begin a special-needs program within a public pre-school. When enrolling Skyler in pre-school, I was informed that according to state funding rules, neither physical therapy (PT) nor occupational therapy (OT) would be offered to Skyler without an official diagnosis of autism; being diagnosed with developmental delay simply wouldn't cut it. My son was still struggling terribly with both fine motor and gross motor skills at this point, and my hands were completely tied until our turn opened up on the autism-diagnosis waitlist.

Skyler had only been in pre-school a month when I finally got the call. It was our turn to be evaluated at the Sarkine Autism Center and get some answers in September 2006. When that day trip to Indianapolis finally came, I was extremely anxious and asking myself ridiculous questions. Did I hope it was "just" autism because the therapeutic treatments are known and easy to implement? What if he didn't have autism but instead had a rare disorder that no one has heard of and, therefore, no one would know how to help him? Could he have significant hearing loss that someone failed to catch during other exams and that's why he doesn't respond to his name? I tried to relax as we parked our car and entered the sterile medical building.

While waiting to see the psychiatrist, I was asked to complete the GARS-2 questionnaire (i.e., the most current Gilliam Autism Rating Scale) so the specialist could gain a better understanding of Skyler's communication, social interaction and demonstration of the stereotypical behaviors associated with autism. Skyler sat comfortably in the hospital-provided red wagon and I got to work. My heart sank deeper into my chest with each "not applicable" bubble I frantically filled in. It was extremely painful to actually read, line by line, all the numerous ways my son was deficient, because it somehow made it more permanent and official ... something was very wrong with my child.

My heart sank deeper into my chest with each "not applicable" bubble I frantically filled in. It was extremely painful to actually read, line by line, all the numerous ways my son was deficient, because it somehow made it more permanent and official ... something was very wrong with my child.

We were finally taken back to the office, which resembled a very small conference room. Unable to sit and chat due to a constant need to redirect Skyler's curious hands from the Kleenex box, file folders and other non-kid-friendly items in the room, I proceeded to rattle off his medical history while in continuous movement. When we saw the visit notes later, all typed up, we read that the physician observed Skyler to be:

> *Extremely hyperactive and inattentive. He repeatedly would spin himself in a circle and did not respond to his name being called. He exhibited significantly decreased eye contact and was noted to repetitively examine the furniture, particularly the chairs in the room. Skyler threw every object presented to him, paced the*

room, and mouthed toys and objects instead of playing with them appropriately.

The exam seemed to last only 20-30 minutes before the doctor turned to me and verified quite confidently that Skyler indeed had autism. My heart shattered into a thousand pieces. I knew, deep down, this was going to be the diagnosis but hearing the statement "your son has autism" from a qualified clinician removed all hope that I was wrong. There was no turning back now. Skyler would forever be labeled as "autistic" — to what degree of severity, we wouldn't yet know. A few additional resources and reading materials were offered to help me wrap my brain around what struggles may lie ahead for us and, just like that, we headed back home with minimal clarity about what to do next.

> **There was no turning back now. Skyler would forever be labeled as "autistic" — to what degree of severity, we wouldn't yet know.**

I held off relaying the news to any family members or friends for a few weeks. I'm not sure why I stayed silent, perhaps solely because I had overwhelming feelings of failure as a mother. I'm sure it's not abnormal to place blame on yourself after a child's diagnosis, but I spent far too much time trying to identify aspects of my pregnancy where I did something wrong. Maybe I shouldn't have eaten tuna those few times because of the mercury. Maybe I exercised too long into the pregnancy. Did even a single Diet Coke's poisonous aspartame cause this? Equally as troubling, I don't think I was ready for the onslaught of questions I couldn't answer or comparisons to the movie *Rain Man*, which would never cease to infuriate me. I beat myself up for my emotional responses at the time, but now — all these years later — I'm at peace with my decision to allow myself the time to cry. Without realizing the value of what I was doing, I allowed

myself to experience the five stages of grief for what I had just lost —
the simple and "normal" life I'd envisioned for my son ... a life that
might never be.

Eventually, I pulled myself together and, with the official autism
diagnosis in hand, started advocating with the school, insurance
companies and local community for immediate resources and treatment options.

Skyler continued experiencing seizures approximately every six
weeks, with a frequency ranging from one per day to multiple per day
for two years. Then, miraculously, at the age of five, as randomly as
the seizure disorder appeared, it stopped! I'm thrilled to report that
Skyler has been seizure-free for the past 12 years.

My Life in Pictures

The famous "tripod" position that Skyler created
for navigating around a room to gather toys

  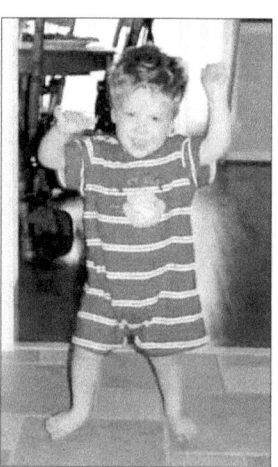

Learning to walk at almost three years of age, the careful and
calculated steps resembling those of Frankenstein's monster

Little Frankenstein's
monster for Halloween

CHAPTER THREE

A Spiritual Journey

I'm often asked by friends and acquaintances, "How do you do it all?" This statement usually comes after someone has observed me when I'm out and about with my two kids in tow, likely trying to redirect Skyler from reaching out to pull someone's beautiful, long hair or smacking the arm of a passerby. What they "know" and who they see is a mother with two teenagers, one with significant special needs, who works a full-time job as a pharmaceutical sales manager and never seems rattled or forgets anything. My response is usually just a smile and shrug of the shoulders, or I dismiss what I assume is meant as a compliment by laughing and saying, "You must've just caught me on a good day." Often, when I describe what a day in our life looks like, people are visibly exhausted just listening to my reality and almost always say, "I could never do it; you are the strongest person I know."

I started really thinking about those words uttered to me thousands of times over the past 17 years. "I could never do it." I reflect back to when I repeatedly said a similar phrase to myself (and to God) when

Skyler was a newly diagnosed toddler: "I can't do this. I don't have the strength or patience."

"I can't do this. I don't have the strength or patience."

I grew up a fiercely devoted Catholic who not only participated in the Sacraments of Initiation — Baptism, Holy Communion and Confirmation — but also attended mass every Sunday morning. Even if I'd spent the night at a friend's house, there was no skipping church. I felt like I had a pretty strong relationship with God throughout my life, although I didn't proactively communicate with him very often. When I received Skyler's diagnosis, I was initially furious at myself, thinking this was somehow my fault, because I had carried him in *my* body. However, my overwhelming anger and frustration then shifted to blaming God. How could he punish me in this way? I've always been a thoughtful and generous person who put others before myself and withstood my own painful childhood growing up the child of an absentee, alcoholic father. Why then would He bless other parents with perfectly healthy children and provide me with this incredibly cruel challenge of raising an imperfect child? I carried on with these beliefs for several years, refused to attend church and practically lost my shit anytime someone reassuringly said, "God only gives you what you can handle." I wanted to scream from the roof-tops, "That's not true because I am not strong enough to handle this!" I was losing my faith.

I had spent my lifetime praying that one day I would have a glorious life characterized by a loving and supportive marriage and beautiful, healthy children. Throughout my pregnancy with Skyler, I daydreamed about what he would look like, the sports or activities he might be involved in and essentially made plans for the next 18 years of his life, only to have it all drastically altered. I mean, honestly, what parent would ever consider an autism diagnosis — or any ailment that significantly impacted their child's life — a "blessing?" I certainly never looked up to the sky and said, "Thank you so much, God, for giving me this incredibly difficult challenge. I'm so gosh darn lucky!" Instead, I would spend many years navigating through seizures, therapies, medications and behavior plans as a divorced mother of two. It was not what I had planned in the slightest, but it was the reality I had accepted.

Despite losing my faith in God, I remained steadfast in believing "everything happens for a reason" and 'when one door closes, another door opens." However, I always found it annoying that the reason for our struggles or the newly opened door wasn't often clear, or didn't happen as fast I would like. After all, I am a planner by nature, and it is frustrating when my plans don't come to fruition how or when I want them to. So, during those very challenging years of single parenting and navigating the world on my own terms, if someone would have told me my faith in God would not only be restored but that I would listen intently to His guidance for my future decisions, I would have laughed hysterically.

In hindsight, I now know that meeting my future husband, Josh, was divine intervention. He entered our lives at a time my family needed him most. Several years post-divorce, I was feeling unfilled in my career, negative about my self-worth, depressed about Skyler's future and dissatisfied overall with my life. During my very first conversation with Josh, I found his positive demeanor and incredible sense of humor to be uplifting. As our relationship became more serious, so did our discussions. The deeply thoughtful perspective and highly spiritual outlook Josh brings to every situation really forced me do some serious soul searching to find clarity in my misdirected anger at God. By reopening my heart and daily dialogue with God, I came to realize that He does not inflict punishment, nor does he make anything imperfect.

By reopening my heart and daily dialogue with God, I came to realize that He does not inflict punishment, nor does he make anything imperfect.

I recognize that fully accepting and understanding the significance of why my child was diagnosed with this confusing and incurable disorder is something that could take a lifetime. Or it's quite possible that I never will truly gain the meaning behind the bigger picture. I now firmly believe that God is using Skyler as a vessel to teach me, and possibly everyone he comes in contact with, some valuable life lessons — patience, gratitude and perhaps an antidote to our societal obsession with perfection. I can definitely say I've grown leaps and bounds emotionally and spiritually during the past 10 years through tons of reflection and prayer, but my journey is not even close to finished. I now fully grasp that God has a plan for me, for Skyler and for our entire family that may or may not ever be revealed to me. He has chosen me to nurture and guide His beloved Skyler through life. The amount of trust He bestowed on me to raise Skyler with an open mind and unconditional love no longer goes unappreciated. Skyler's determination is unsurpassed and consistently teaches us how to find enjoyment in the simplest things.

I thank God each day for ensuring my path crossed with Josh at just the right time — on God's time and according to His plan. Josh was the guiding light back to my faith and encouraged me to lean back into the arms of God. By opening up my heart and mind to allow God's direction and guidance for my life and Skyler's life to take shape, I've found true joy in the daily blessings, big and small. Being Skyler's mom makes me extremely proud, and I am forever grateful to God for entrusting me with this precious and admirable son.

Just recently, a close friend sent me the following poem entitled "The Special Mother," authored in 1983 by American humorist Erma Bombeck.[1] I believe it explains precisely how I now feel about my amazing blessing, Skyler.

Did you ever wonder how mothers of handicapped children are chosen?

Somehow, I visualize God hovering over Earth selecting His instruments for propagation with great care and deliberation. As He observes, He instructs His angels to make notes in a giant ledger:

"Armstrong, Beth, son. Patron saint, Matthew.

"Forest, Marjorie, daughter. Patron saint, Cecelia.

"Rutledge, Carrie, twins. Patron saint ... give her Gerard. He's used to profanity."

Finally, He passes a name to an angel and smiles, "Give her a handicapped child."

The angel is curious. "Why this one, God? She's so happy."

"Exactly," smiles God. "Could I give a handicapped child to a mother who does not know laughter? That would be cruel."

"But has she patience?" asks the angel.

"I don't want her to have too much patience, or she will drown in a sea of self-pity and despair. Once the shock and resentment wear off, she'll handle it.

---

1   Erma Bombeck, *Motherhood: The Second Oldest Profession*, Open Road Media, 2013 Kindle Edition, eBook Location 805.

"I watched her today. She has that sense of self and independence that are so rare and so necessary in a mother. You see, the child I'm giving to her has his own world. She has to make it live in her world and that's not going to be easy."

"But Lord, I don't think she even believes in you."

God smiles. "No matter, I can fix that. This one is perfect. She has just enough selfishness."

The angel gasps. "Selfishness? Is that a virtue?"

God nods. "If she can't separate herself from the child occasionally, she'll never survive. Yes, here is a woman whom I will bless with a child less than perfect. She doesn't realize it yet, but she is to be envied.

"She will never take for granted a spoken word. She will never consider a step ordinary. When her child says 'Momma' for the first time, she will be witness to a miracle and know it ...

"I will permit her to see clearly the things I see — ignorance, cruelty, prejudice — and allow her to rise above them. She will never be alone. I will be at her side every minute of every day of her life because she is doing my work as surely as she is here by my side."

"And what about her Patron saint?" asks the angel, his pen poised in mid-air.

God smiles. "A mirror will suffice."

CHAPTER FOUR

The Evolution of a Family Dynamic

Divorce is never easy, particularly when you're going through it while raising two small children, one of whom has significant delays (and to what degree we were not yet certain at that time). The physical relocation of parents into separate residences, the division of belongings and the creation of shared custody schedules takes quite a toll on everyone. However, even with all that in mind, the decision to divorce came fairly easily to me. When putting a magnifying glass over the relationship with my first husband, it was clear that I was essentially a "single parent" living with a roommate instead of a husband. We had almost nothing in common; we were polar opposites. And while opposites sometime attract, they don't always stick together when life gets real. He was an introverted homebody, and I was an extroverted social butterfly who used marathon running as my outlet for stress. I tried to make it work, suggesting we go to counseling. It was a suggestion he dismissed while continuing to live in denial. So I sought out a therapist to work through my feelings of sadness and anger — the sadness I felt living in a loveless marriage and the anger I harbored with the world because of this damn autism diagnosis.

In the fall of 2008, which turned out to be the last year of our 10-year marriage, I had a wakeup call and knew I needed to move on with my life while I was still young (mid-30s seems super young to me now!). I knew I needed to provide a more loving and supportive environment for the kids to thrive. The "wakeup call" was literally a wakeup call. I awoke one Saturday morning to my daughter, Kendall, leaping into my bed to snuggle. After spending about 15 minutes with me she said, "I'm going to go downstairs to Daddy's room and wake him up now!" That statement hit me like a ton of bricks. My 3-year-old daughter thought it was normal for parents to have separate bedrooms. Sadly, that was our arrangement the last three years of our marriage, so it is all she had ever known. This wasn't the life I wanted — for me, or for my children.

Shared Custody and Single Parenthood

The one part of being divorced that I didn't anticipate was the extreme loneliness when the kids were "at their dad's," which is also a phrase that became as normal to say as "how are you?" My kids are my everything, so not knowing every detail of their day crushed my heart. I played the enabling ex-wife role for several years post-divorce. I picked up all of Skyler's medicines, with dual pill bottles, so each home would have a supply. I scheduled all appointments. I purchased the kid's clothes and shoes for his home because "he didn't know their sizes," etc. His family also made it easy for him to not be a completely invested dad by visiting from out of state every other weekend to help him "watch" the kids and bringing him homemade food to last the entire week (because he also didn't like to cook). I was a single parent (working full-time and with occasional help from a babysitter) and he was a parent with lots and lots of support. For him, "it took a village."

The week-on/week-off custody schedule slowly became my new normal, and I embraced it, knowing that I was a strong, capable and amazing mom warrior. I believe we each have a warrior inside of us, and it doesn't take much to rile that fighting spirit of a mamma bear — especially when it involves her children. I'm fully aware that kids at any age can embellish situations to fulfill their own agendas. When my daughter would come back from her dad's house, she would be the voice for her non-verbal, older brother and wanted to share every detail. I made it a point to not ask questions outside of "What did you do last week for fun? Did your brother eat? How was school?" etc. because I didn't want her to worry that she was tattling or sharing forbidden, personal intel on her dad. She would tell me that she didn't see her brother much because he was napping a lot or spent time in his room in the basement. It was concerning to me that he did not have interaction with everyone and that he was alone "sleeping" a lot. That would be the first of many topics that triggered arguments with my ex-husband about Skyler's welfare during "daddy weekends."

> **I believe we each have a warrior inside of us, and it doesn't take much to rile that fighting spirit of a mamma bear — especially when it involves her children.**

I, on the other hand, was doing okay. Despite having no family living in the same state as me to offer an occasional hand, single parenting was going well. I honestly enjoyed living on my own and doing things *my* way. And the kids were doing well, too.

I made just one big post-divorce mistake, and that one we'll file under "the perils of rebound dating." Shortly after becoming single, I got into a relationship that turned out to be abusive and toxic — a relationship with a man who had loose standards when it came to telling the truth, staying sober and practicing monogamy. I got out quickly and learned a lot. In fact, I'm actually grateful for that experience because it taught me just how resilient and independent I can be. It was that post-divorce, rebound relationship that would forge the path to meeting my soulmate.

Finding "the One"

One summer Saturday morning, I was running at a local park and bumped into a former work acquaintance who was also an avid runner. We talked for a minute and shared contact information before continuing on with our respective mileage. A few conversations over text led me to ask, somewhat jokingly, if he had any single friends — because the dating pool around town was, from my experience, full of many unsavory characters and I could use a good recommendation. My friend informed me that one guy in particular from his running group, Josh, came to his mind right away, and he was pretty certain of Josh's single status. Just like in middle school — when we passed "notes" instead of texts and emails — my friend accepted the role of matchmaker and spoke with "runner-guy Josh," telling him a little bit about me to gauge his interest. The feedback I later received was that Josh had been burned several times in the recent past and was essentially taking a break from dating. Go figure.

My friend said it was up to me to reach out to Josh, if I was interested, because he was *not* going to pursue anyone right now. *Um, what?* At first, I thought, *"Is this what dating is like now? It's been quite a while since I've been in the game and, man, things have sure changed!"* My second thought was, *"Who in the hell is this guy and why does he think I'm desperate enough to proactively contact him, knowing he may or may not respond?"* As it turns out, I was, indeed, desperate enough — Ha! I sure as hell wasn't joining any more dating apps, so, challenge accepted.

Like any good researcher (aka stalker) doing her due diligence before deciding to meet this dude, I looked through his profile on Facebook, of course, because that's where people put their best photos and share evidence of living their best lives right? And I decided to message him. From that day on, we probably exchanged 50 texts a day for weeks before deciding to meet up for lunch. He was hilarious, confident but not cocky, more sarcastic than me (which I didn't think was even possible), handsome, exactly one day older than me, and seemed to bring very little proverbial baggage. That first lunch was the beginning of our fairytale. Our lunch conversation flowed so easily, like we had known each other our entire lives. At one point, he even casually teased that he was on pace to win a fabulous trip to Italy from his employer, and if I "played my cards right," I may get to tag along. I'm sure you're thinking exactly what I was thinking at the time: *"Is this guy for real? What is he hiding? And why hasn't he been married?"*

The relationship progressed very easily, and I was pinching myself as a reminder that this was absolutely real. When my friends and family first met Josh, they all said the same thing, "What an amazing guy!" As I said prior, I honestly give all the credit to God for bringing us together. Aside from all the other amazing qualities Josh possesses, I fell completely in love with him while watching him interact with my kids. After a few months of dating, I invited him over one evening to have dinner with me and the kids. I had made it perfectly clear that I come as a package deal. If you are unaccepting of or act uncomfortable around my children, especially Skyler, we're done. When Josh arrived that night for dinner, I didn't even get the chance to slowly ease him into my house because Skyler walked right up to him, grabbed his hand and led him to the basement to show him some toys. Kendall was super shy, but she warmed up to Josh quickly, as well, because he made her laugh and seemed so comfortable being silly.

I had made it perfectly clear that I come as a package deal. If you are unaccepting of or act uncomfortable around my children, especially Skyler, we're done.

About a year into our relationship, Josh did earn that company-sponsored vacation to Italy that he jokingly dangled over my head and, thankfully, chose to take me. That trip would change the future for all of us and would mark the beginning of our new family. Completely taken by surprise, I turned around from making a wish in the Trevi Fountain in Rome, to see Josh on one knee with a ring box in his hand. I was in utter shock but excitedly said "yes" to his teary-eyed marriage proposal. Our wedding occurred a little over a year later with both kids acting as an integral part of the festivities — walking me down the aisle and participating in the unity sand ceremony. Skyler even entertained the crowd with his partner dancing with Josh and me at the reception.

Josh and Skyler, dancing at our wedding reception

Family time — tearing up the dance floor

Kendall and Skyler, proudly walking
their mom down the aisle

Skyler's Father Shows His True Colors

From the beginning of our relationship, Josh has expressed so much love for both kids and has been their biggest cheerleader and supporter — wanting to be involved in everything, like an amazing bonus dad should. When my ex would make poor decisions, mostly driven by spite toward me, causing suffering to the kids, Josh was equally as emotional but somewhat afraid to overstep his bounds. One incident, in particular, was about as emotional as it can get when it comes to a new couple coping with the drama and interpersonal toxicity of engaging with an ex-spouse and co-parent. There's no sugar-coated way to tell this story, nor do I want to belabor it or vilify any participants, so I'll share just the facts. When Skyler was 9 years old, his biological dad suggested that Skyler undergo surgical castration to keep him small in overall physical stature. My ex emailed me out of the blue and said of Skyler:

> *Currently he is small, but as he gets bigger and hits puberty, I think he will change significantly. He will not only get bigger and stronger but will have more aggression issues. When this occurs, it is very likely we will not be able to keep him in our homes for our safety and his. There are some things that can be done to keep him small and to stop puberty from starting. They are not easy to discuss, but it might be in Skyler's best long-term interest and will increase the likelihood that he can remain in our homes. I do think we need to meet and discuss this.*

At this point, my ex-husband was also remarried to a woman who had been openly cruel to Skyler, and any discussion of puberty took me aback because our very tiny 9-year-old had the physicality of a 5-year-old. I read and re-read the email several times with Josh and asked if he would attend the meeting with me. Of course, he said he definitely would be there. I suggested to my ex that he bring his wife along, so we could make parenting decisions, whatever they turned out to be, as a team. He showed up without her.

We met in the parking lot of Kendall's gymnastics class, and I waited for him to lay out his "research" and his master plan to stop the hitting of people and banging on walls that Skyler exhibited much more frequently at my ex's home. I was in no way prepared for him to lead with "I found a way to halt puberty."

I gasped and looked at him with fire in my eyes before angrily exclaiming, "Come again? Why would we want to halt puberty and how would that stop the hitting/banging?" He went on to explain that if Skyler were to be castrated, he would stay small and therefore not hit as hard or grow to a size that we couldn't manage to care for him.

My eyes instantly welled up with tears at the very thought of my sweet, innocent, little boy enduring an unnecessary surgery — something that struck me as barbaric and inhumane — all to supposedly make his dad's life easier and quieter. I looked over at Josh's shocked face and lost my self-control. In no uncertain terms, I told my ex that he should be ashamed of himself, and that he needed to learn how to be a damn parent. There are reasons Skyler bangs — for attention, to express pain or distress, if he's hungry. Our job as his parents is to nurture, protect and guide him through all of it. This "meeting" was over.

Over time, it became more and more clear to me that Skyler's time with his father and his father's wife was more harmful than loving, and I became very concerned. By my ex-husband's choice, Skyler was often isolated and had been excluded from so many "family" activities: family trips to the grandparents' home to celebrate Thanksgiving and Christmas year after year (I frequently received an email saying "Skyler will not be making the trip this year, so would you be able to take him for the holiday weekend?"); Florida vacations; restaurants;

his sister's dance recitals; or running errands. He was always segregated, alone in the basement where his was the only bedroom. Then I learned that my ex had crafted a 15-foot by 15-foot exercise pen (i.e., cage) made of short, iron fencing with a flooring layer of recycled tires in his backyard as a way of "letting Skyler play outside!" Skyler's box was absent of toys, other than one large rubber ball, and was located only feet away from the swing set my ex's toddler daughter played on. Skyler watched others run and play freely around the yard while he was caged up like a dog. In my opinion, it was complete mental and emotional abuse. Skyler was living a life of isolation every other week and, based on our custody arrangement, there wasn't a damn thing I could do about it. Not surprisingly, Skyler's banging and hitting increased in my ex's home; I imagine it's because he was desperate for affection and attention.

I knew it was a matter of time before the next "serious" business-like email regarding Skyler would come from my ex. Late in 2016, Skyler was age 13. I received an email stating, "I believe it's time we start discussing Skyler's present and future." That struck me as some heavy talk from someone who didn't appear to give a shit about his son's present. He went on, "I feel it would be in Skyler's best interest to have one parent making all the decisions and also one primary home where he spends most of the time, so his day-to-day life is more consistent." Ironically, I practically begged — since the castration suggestion years before — for Skyler to live primarily with me but was always met with "not a chance." I think he feared having to pay child support, if that happened. So, this email came as a welcome surprise, and I thought, *"Finally he agrees with me that I provide a more stable home for Skyler."* I'm getting what I want and Skyler gets what he deserves — a family who loves him and engages with him.

Weeks of embittered back-and-forth communication on my ex-husband's position regarding Skyler's living arrangements included a brief suggestion that he be the primary custodial parent, that Skyler be more heavily medicated and that Skyler lose the benefit of his behavioral therapy at the Autism Center. It all felt like a twisted emotional game to me.

Ultimately, Skyler's dad suggested that his visitations with his son include just one 36-hour period per month, and two non-consecutive weeks in the summer. He wanted to keep his regular bi-weekly visitation schedule with our neurotypical daughter, Kendall. And he suggested that no child-support monies be due to me because "having Skyler should be its own reward." Ahem.

I was overcome with frustration but did my best to focus on what my children needed and deserved. I spent some time thinking through everything and really looking at what was best for Kendall and Skyler both. The kids deserve the healthiest relationship possible with both parents and I worried about what this might do to Kendall, because she and her brother have always gone to their dad's together every other week. I also was concerned that Skyler would forget who his dad is, only seeing him one overnight a month.

We eventually arrived at a verbal agreement for a revised custody arrangement. Soon after the verbal agreement was reached and while my attorney was working on the Agreed Order of Modification for Skyler's custody, Josh and I decided that it was very important to sit down with Kendall and explain the situation. She was almost 12 and had been adhering to the same schedule as her brother for the past eight years; so, in my opinion, she had every right to know about the major changes about to happen. I posed the question to her this way: "How would you feel if your brother didn't go with you to your dad's house every other week but instead lived here permanently and only visited there one weekend a month?"

Her first response was, "It's about time." (She's always been a smart cookie and straight shooter!) Following that remark, demonstrating her typical selfless and empathetic nature, she said, "That would be so great for Buddy, to stay here with you and Josh." I explained to her that her dad agrees that it is in Skyler's best interest to live pretty much full-time with me. She asked about the timeline, and I told her it would be effective as soon as we can get the agreement signed by the judge.

The new custody arrangement was put into place the week of Thanksgiving in 2016. That first week of Kendall going to her dad's without her brother was approaching and, up to this point, Josh and I were the only adults who had communicated anything about the situation to her. Kendall's dad, according to Kendall, explained the situation to her like this: "Your brother is going to live most of the time with your mom. But don't worry, we aren't getting rid of you too. We're keeping you." His words and behaviors broke my heart at every turn, but my kids are amazingly resilient. And life was taking positive turns, despite the pain experienced to get to this juncture.

The Financial Realties

We were six months into the new custody arrangement, and life was great. The only thing that would've made life even more amazing would have been having Kendall live with us 95% of the time, too. But we all understood that wasn't going to happen. Skyler was thriving with a familiar routine, and it was easy to see that he enjoyed the familiarity of sleeping in the same bed, eating at the same dinner table, and taking a bath in the same bathtub every single night. Sadly, I think we all failed to recognize how confusing the weekly switch had been for him all these years and took for granted how important consistency can be. However, one area that started becoming inconsistent for Skyler was his "school," which was a program at an autism center that offered one-to-one applied behavior analysis (ABA) therapy all day with teachers/therapists specializing in children with autism.

Skyler was thriving with a familiar routine, and it was easy to see that he enjoyed the familiarity of sleeping in the same bed, eating at the same dinner table, and taking a bath in the same bathtub every single night.

Skyler had been attending this program for approximately seven years and had gained so many skills, while also nearly eliminating those behaviors that were problematic: hair pulling, frequent hitting and never *ever* sitting down. The director of the center, Lauren — who we adored so much and considered a part of our family (she was even Skyler's "date" … a.k.a. babysitter … at our wedding) — announced she was stepping away from her position and moving to Switzerland. We were devastated. Not only because Skyler had a major crush on her, but because we knew she was always there to look out for him when we were not. The trust with therapists and caregivers takes such a long time to build, and we were concerned Lauren's bond with Skyler couldn't be replaced.

I started researching other programs in Kentucky, where Skyler's current center was, and on our side of the Ohio River in Indiana. At the same time, Josh and I decided to once again seek out a behavioral therapist to assist with some of the troublesome behaviors Skyler still exhibited in our home. During my meeting with the company who provided the therapists, the director mentioned they would soon be opening an ABA center like the one Skyler was currently attending in Kentucky, but much closer to our home in Indiana. I looked up to the ceiling and smiled at God. I was witnessing His divine intervention into my life yet again. Even better than that, the hefty $35,000 annual tuition we were paying completely out of pocket for the Kentucky program would now cost us *absolutely nothing* because our health insurance, combined with Skyler's Indiana Medicaid waiver, would finally be put to extraordinarily good use.

Part of my original divorce agreement stipulated that, in lieu of child support, my ex-husband would cover 75% of Skyler's tuition expense at the Autism Center in Kentucky. However, being awarded both physical and legal guardianship afforded me the authority to make all decisions regarding his health and well-being, which included schooling and therapy selections. I thought my ex would be elated that I located a facility not only much closer to home, but that provided more hours of the ABA therapy we both wanted for our son (equating to approximately $100,000 per year) on a year-round schedule, completely covered by insurance. I sent him a courtesy email the minute I knew, letting him know when Skyler would be changing ABA centers, so he could stop making payments to the prior facility. I requested that he continue paying the same monthly fee he was paying for tuition but asked that he pay it into the Special Needs Trust I had set up for Skyler. (I was advised many years ago to create a Special Needs Trust, which Josh and I fund monthly, to ensure there will be ample funds for Skyler's future needs. It provides more safety than a traditional bank account because it is untouchable by anyone who may attempt to take advantage of Skyler or his money.)

> **I was advised many years ago to create a Special Needs Trust, which Josh and I fund monthly, to ensure there will be ample funds for Skyler's future needs.**

I naively assumed my ex-husband would like that idea, because it meant that money was *not* going to me in the form of any child support, but that it would be helping secure funding for

Skyler's future needs. You know what they say about people who "assume." He replied, "Thank you for allowing me the opportunity to contribute to your trust; however, I do not see the need to contribute funds to your trust for Skyler. As long as I am working, I can handle the current funding myself through my own savings plan. I am very aware of Skyler's need for funds during his life and I will always be here to help."

So it appeared he expected me and Josh to provide, emotionally and physically, for Skyler's every need, with the exception of 12 nights a year, and expected us to financially support 100% of Skyler's daily needs for his lifetime too. The mom warrior in me went into high gear once again, and I called my attorney. As expected, I was advised that Skyler and Kendall's dad absolutely can't refuse to support his children. Because we no longer owed monthly tuition, and my ex-husband refused to work with me on an alternative arrangement, I had no choice but to take him back to court for child support. What a long, drawn-out and emotional battle this would become.

> **I had no choice but to take him back to court for child support. What a long, drawn-out and emotional battle this would become.**

The challenge began by his refusal to turn over his tax returns to my attorney, which are needed so child support can be calculated. His attorneys argued that until ordered by a judge to comply with our request, the tax returns would not be released. The judge took only minutes to issue the order and we finally received the information, although it was conveniently a "draft" copy with many redactions. Instead of a judge's ruling for support, we settled on a mediation, which was scheduled and rescheduled several times. I was beginning to think there would be no end to this mess.

I Adopt a New Attitude and Josh Adopts a Son

As irritating as these many months of shenanigans were, I never lost sight of the very sad bigger picture. The only person my ex was hurting in all of this was his son. Growing tired of the numerous delays and becoming broke from attorney's fees, I asked my attorney her thoughts on dropping the child support motion and, instead, pursuing a step-parent adoption at the mediation. She asked if I was serious about proceeding with that option and, without hesitation, I practically screamed "ABSOLUTELY!" It had never been about the money; it had everything to do with me wanting my ex to be a good father and to support his son in some capacity. Because he was emotionally unavailable to Skyler, it was reasonable to expect him to at least contribute financially to his care. But even that wasn't worth fighting for forever. We needed to move forward in a healing way. I wanted everyone to see me, Josh, Skyler and Kendall as the family we were. It occurred to me that there was a wonderful way to do this.

The bond between Josh and Skyler is like nothing I've ever seen. Many people jokingly call Josh "the Skyler whisperer" because he can literally get Skyler to do anything and Josh brings a constant smile to Skyler's face. When I approached Josh about the possibility of becoming Skyler's dad, his eyes welled up and he said, "That would mean the world to me. I love that little guy so much."

As with the prior situation of full custody, I felt it would be best to discuss this with Kendall. Josh and I waited until we had a quiet, private moment with her, when Skyler was tucked into bed for the evening. We all snuggled on the couch for our typical Saturday movie night but before starting the movie, we asked Kendall if we could talk to her about the upcoming mediation and get her thoughts on one particular subject. She tilted her head, a look of concern plastered across her face, and asked if she was in some sort of trouble. We assured her that we only wanted her honest opinion about something that concerned Skyler but that would impact her too. I proceeded to ask how she would feel if Josh became Skyler's dad through adoption.

I'll never ever forget her smile and response, which was, "That's so great! Josh is more of a dad to him anyway and that would be amazing for Buddy." Josh wanted to make sure she fully understood that he loves her equally as much and that would never change regardless of a last name. Kendall said she knew that and was really happy for Skyler. We answered more of her questions but further explained that it was likely a long shot that it would happen but, just in case her dad agreed to Josh adopting Skyler, we didn't want her to find out after the fact and feel upset that no one cared enough to talk to her first.

The day of the mediation, I felt sick to my stomach. He would never agree to a step-parent adoption … or would he? I can say with the utmost confidence that the majority of his decisions are financially motivated, so maybe there was a chance. The mediator came into our room first, and my attorney informed her that we didn't want to get into a back-and-forth game with the child support figure and battle about misrepresented income amounts. My attorney had come prepared with the step-parent adoption form ready to be signed. The mediator thought it would be best to find out the monthly number they were prepared to offer for support and if we were as far apart as she assumed we would be, she would present the adoption option to them. As predicted, our support numbers were so far apart you could park a Greyhound bus between them. Now was the moment of truth. The mediator was going to ask him to relinquish his parental rights.

I waited for what seemed like an eternity. The mediator, straight-faced, walked back into our room and actually appeared a bit shocked herself when she said the words that are forever cemented in my memory: "He agreed to it." I stared at her blankly and then finally struggled to spit out the words, "Agreed to the adoption?" Yes, he agreed to relinquish all rights so Josh could become Skyler's legal father. Wow. As thrilled as I was that this outcome — an outcome I wanted so badly — had finally happened, the fact that my ex made the decision so quickly also made me extremely sad for Skyler. Although Skyler has a much stronger bond and loving relationship with Josh than with his biological father, I couldn't help but worry about the ramifications this decision would have on Kendall (as well as the members of my ex's family who weren't consulted — by virtue of this decision, Skyler's aunts, uncles, cousins, step-sister, half-sister and grandparents all stood to lose a regular connection with our son, and I knew that some of them would be heartbroken).

The mediator asked my ex when he would like the change to be made, and apparently he requested to sign the order immediately if it was available right then. The step-parent adoption consent form was signed on the spot, and after a few other topics were addressed regarding Kendall, the mediation was over, and I rushed home to tell Josh the amazing news.

During the entire drive home, I was overcome with varying emotions. Still in disbelief, I was rehashing the entire outcome out loud while my facial expressions transitioned between giggles with a plastered smile and uncontrollable sobbing. Cars positioned next to me at the stop lights probably thought I was losing my mind. I glanced at my phone, noting all the missed calls from family members who were on pins and needles waiting for me to reveal the outcome, but knew this was too important to simply mention over the phone to anyone before Josh was told.

I pulled into our garage and couldn't get through the door fast enough. I threw open the door and yelled the amazing news in the form of a traditional birth announcement, "Congratulations, Dad! It's a five-foot, four-inch, 125-pound, 16-year-old boy!"

Adoption Day! Our family photo with Magistrate Joni Grayson. Kendall was eager to attend this very important day for her big brother.

Josh's eyes flooded with tears. He was over the moon with excitement and was thrilled that Skyler would officially be his son, even sharing his last name; however, in his mind, this didn't change anything with the relationship already between them. Josh had spent the past seven years tending to Skyler's every need and was fully invested as his dad on every level; this was just a legal formality. But it was still mighty special. The mediation day fell on a week Kendall was with my ex, so she hurried home after dance class to FaceTime with me. I asked her if her dad had any conversation with her about the outcome of our meeting, so I could gauge what she already knew from his version of events. According to Kendall, he said, "Sometimes you have to make hard decisions in life" and that he was forced to let Skyler live with me full time. I told her, "I was honestly shocked that he actually agreed to it, too!"

Kendall, not clear at that point that Skyler "living with us full time" meant that her dad agreed to a step-parent adoption, looked at me, stunned and said, "Wait, what? Did he give up Skyler for adoption?" The impact of her chosen words "give up" wasn't lost on me. I explained that yes, her dad signed the papers for Josh to adopt Skyler, and the arrangement would be effective immediately.

I didn't elaborate on this point with Kendall, but my ex did ask during the mediation that he still be allowed to see Skyler the last Sunday of each month from 10:00 a.m. to 7:00 p.m. I was quite adamant that Skyler would only be confused by an infrequent visit such as that, and I would prefer that all ties be severed. My attorney advised that he could pull the adoption from the table, and we would be back to arguing over child support numbers, if I gave a firm no on any type of visitation, so I reluctantly agreed. It's really not in Skyler's best interest to keep sending him over to his biological father's house, but I felt like I was between a rock and a hard place. What could I do? Kendall was truly excited for Skyler and jokingly said, "What about me? Can Josh adopt me too?" It was a sweet and supportive question, which broke my heart a little too ... because I know there was an element of true need in her question. This is exactly why we discussed it with her months before, in preparation for this outcome and so she would always know that nothing about her relationship with Josh would change. In the course of that conversation, she moved from happiness for Skyler to anger with her dad. She was furious that he never mentioned adoption to her and glossed over the permanency of it, implying that what happened at the mediation was really just about residential custody. The following week, when Kendall returned home, I was peppered with questions and her concerns that if she does something wrong, "Is he gonna get rid of me too?"

After the adoption news had been shared with Josh, our family members and close friends, it dawned on me that my ex's parents might be left wondering about their grandparent status in Skyler's life. Being that I still have a close relationship with my former mother-in-law, I guess I was hoping that she would proactively reach out to me to express her feelings regarding the adoption. When I didn't hear anything a few days post mediation, I decided to reach out to her via text, which I now recognize was probably not the best way to communicate. I cowardly chose that method out of fear that, per usual, my ex had cast me as the villain who hoodwinked him into giving up his child. I explained in my message that despite her son's decision to allow Josh to adopt Skyler, absolutely nothing about her relationship with her grandson would change. I concluded that I know how much she loves both Kendall and Skyler and I would never do anything to harm those relationships.

My mind wandered over the several hours as I waited for her to respond. I wondered: *"Is she angry with me? Does she know about the adoption? Surely my ex told his parents about this major life event, right?"*

Well, as I would come to find out, he did *not* share the mediation outcome with his parents. The first they heard about it was from me and they were devastated. Unbelievable — it was the only word that came to mind. I was beyond shocked that he didn't feel it necessary to share this change of family dynamic with his daughter or his parents. They love Skyler too. I can only imagine how they were feeling.

My former in-laws continue to have a strong bond with Skyler and Kendall, which Josh and I encourage with open invitations to see us anytime. Witnessing Skyler's smiles and interaction with his grandparents during a recent visit reinforces to me that Josh and I have our priorities focused in the right place — on the best interest of our kids and the entire family who loves them.

CHAPTER FIVE

All the Treatments

At the onset of our Autism diagnosis, the well-paved path to a tried-and-true treatment plan was non-existent. So, when I was offered books, medical professionals, connections to parents with children on the spectrum, various therapy styles and gobs of opinions, I accepted it all with an open mind. However, with each new treatment or potential "cure" that comes to light, parents are forced to weigh the risks versus rewards. Oftentimes, new programs and treatments reduce our children's symptoms and behaviors into a one-size-fits-all approach. It should come as no surprise that these unrealistic promises for successful results and dramatic changes in our children are not met. False hope is a dangerous thing for a family like mine. It's emotionally and financially devastating for a family to start and stop so many new "medical breakthroughs." Time and again, nothing really works. And the fads and promises exploit the desperation of parents who feel a sense of urgency to find a treatment that will finally help their children realize their fullest potentials and live independent lives.

At the onset of our Autism diagnosis, the well-paved path to a tried-and-true treatment plan was non-existent. So, when I was offered books, medical professionals, connections to parents with children on the spectrum, various therapy styles and gobs of opinions, I accepted it all with an open mind.

Keeping all those things in mind from the start, my philosophy has always been to try interventions that have plenty of medical evidence to demonstrate a benefit as long as the treatments inflicted no pain or harm to Skyler. The most frustrating aspect of all the treatment philosophies introduced to me over the years (besides feeling scammed by exaggerated testimonials) has been the false hope I would inevitably conjure on each treatment journey — sure that "this approach" would finally be the turning point for Skyler. Taking to heart claims that these "breakthrough" therapies or medicines positively improved the speech or cognition of other children made it that much more heartbreaking each time not a single benefit was visible with Skyler. I felt despair after despair.

Nutrition and Supplements and Horses, Oh My!

My laundry list of treatments began with the gluten-free/casein-free (GF/CF) diet. The theory presented by some of the medical community at the time suggested that gluten (a protein found in wheat and other grains) and casein (a protein found in cow's milk/dairy) were often poorly absorbed by children on the autism spectrum because they had compromised immune systems and many had "leaky gut syndrome." The theory suggested that ingesting gluten and casein caused gastrointestinal inflammation, which took a toll on brain function, resulting in anxiety, mood abnormalities and mental diffi-culties — and would, perhaps, in the case of children and adults on the spectrum, worsen the behavioral symptoms of autism. Based on this "science," I made weekly, expensive trips to Whole Foods, where I purchased everything I could find with GF/CF on the label that looked like something a child might eat. Fish sticks, chicken nuggets, loaves of GF bread, crackers, cookies, etc. I will say that GF foods have come a long way since then but, at the time, most of it tasted and felt like cardboard — dry and without flavor. Skyler was three years old when he began the strict GF/CF diet and maintained it for two years. There weren't any noticeable changes in his behaviors, eye contact or digestion, so I slowly introduced gluten back into his diet to see if maybe there were some identifiable benefits that perhaps I was over-looking. There weren't. (In the long run, however, Skyler liked most of the gluten-free foods we were feeding him, and I'm gluten-intolerant, so we've remained a relatively gluten-free family. The casein came back into his diet, without incidence.)

After all our experi-ments with what Skyler was eating, we started exploring how he was moving. I believe it was Skyler's physical therapist who first mentioned the concept of hippotherapy to me. (Horses, not hippos!) The idea is to utilize

Skyler with his horse friend
during hippotherapy

equine movement as a therapy tool to engage sensory, neuromotor and cognitive systems to promote functional outcomes in children or adults with developmental delays or impairments. And watching tiny Skyler at the age of three on that huge horse was about the cutest thing I've ever seen! He seemed to enjoy it, and the horses were extremely helpful with calming his need for constant movement. The facility had a big arena for horse riding, and also had a large therapy room with lots of sensory equipment — swings, hammocks and various textured toys. Although Skyler seemed to enjoy his hourly appointment each week, after a year, I was seeing very little improvement with his fine or gross motor skills and the 45-minute drive each way to the barn was exhausting for both of us. Equally as frustrating was the constant refusal by the insurance company to cover this "unnecessary" and "experimental" therapy billed under the autism diagnosis codes. So, I made the decision to halt this therapy and move on to something that would perhaps show some more tangible growth and improvement.

It's become a rite of passage for autism families to have to address the theories or beliefs associated with autism and vaccines. I'm not about to use this forum to tackle the issue of whether vaccines play a role in the development of autism, but I will say that the controversial conversations happening in this regard reached a fever pitch at the time of Skyler's diagnosis and brought more attention to this growing disorder. All I was focused on at the time was helping my son continue to improve. While I was chatting with a few autism moms at a local parent support group (which I had joined early in this journey), the discussion arose about one particular specialist who several of their children were seeing. I guess it was apparent by the puzzled look on my face that I had no idea what they were talking about. Their response was pure shock that, at the age of five, Skyler was not being treated by a "DAN doctor." A what?

Once again, I felt like a horrible mom because I hadn't heard of "DAN doctors." It sounded like a secret physician society. It turns out that DAN was founded in 1995 and stood for Defeat Autism Now. Providers labeled with this classification were trained in the DAN protocol, which starts with the idea that autism is a biomedical condition (i.e., that it's not just a mental difference but a brain disease that could benefit from treatment). The focus is based strongly in the possibility that autism could be cured through biomedical interventions ranging from nutritional therapy and supplements to removal of heavy metals from the body (i.e., chelation) and hyperbaric oxygen treatment (HBOT).

It all sounded very intriguing to me and it appeared that, to be a better autism warrior mom, it was a requirement for me to get smart and get on top of this. So I located the closest DAN physician near us (who happened to be in Ohio) and I scheduled an appointment. Just like every other autism resource facility, this medical practice had a wait list that was almost a year long. As I had done previously while awaiting Skyler's diagnosis, I researched as much as I could and spoke with other parents whose children were patients of this particular DAN physician. And when our appointment finally arrived, I soaked up every word of what he counseled, and Skyler left there with a lengthy list of supplements to begin taking, as well as a very costly hyperbaric oxygen chamber (also called "an HBOT" by people in the know) to use at home, courtesy of his loving and supportive grandfather. The HBOT proved interesting because it

required me getting inside of it with Skyler for our 45-minute daily sessions. I was a single mother at that time, so I had to teach my little 4-year-old daughter Kendall how to zip it closed and let us out when the time was over. Despite all the feedback from other

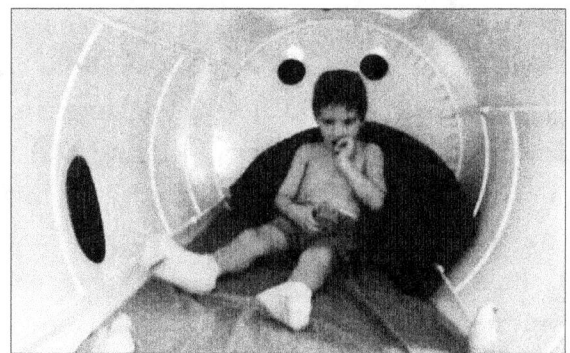

Skyler and Laurie inside the hyperbaric oxygen chamber for one of many HBOT treatments

families whose children remarkably became verbal after using the supplements and HBOT, yet again, after two years, I saw no noticeable changes with Skyler, so I discontinued all of it. I've since learned, when researching for this book, the DAN protocol was discontinued in 2011 due, in large part, to the false claim associated in the name "defeat" autism. While many parents claim the DAN protocol anecdotally "cured" their children, there is essentially no evidence or peer-reviewed research to support this.

Medications, Treatments and Tests

Not one to pause or pout for very long after a setback, I moved to a new set of experiments. We would begin some behavioral medications for Skyler, with the goal of helping him focus and actually sit down for more than 3-second increments at his autism center. The pediatrician prescribed a few initial medications but was not comfortable with prescribing and managing psychiatric medicines (e.g., antidepressants, anti-anxiety medications, stimulants for ADHD) to young children long-term, so we were referred to a child psychiatrist who specialized in autism.

Between the ages of seven and nine, at my reluctance, Skyler was placed on several cocktails of medications and none were very successful. In addition, he started demonstrating some potentially irreversible side effects (akathisia and tics), and some of his behaviors worsened, so I was no longer feeling this path was in his best interest. The appointments with this autism psychiatry group offered us little to no help, and they were expensive, as our insurance would only reimburse a small portion of my self-submitted claims. (This is the period of time where I bestowed upon myself an honorary degree in insurance-claim navigation and their respective appellate processes.) We severed ties with the group and transferred to a family practice physician who was not only a member of our church, but who was the mother of twin teenage boys who both have autism. Considering that she could relate to the highs and lows of parenting children on the spectrum, she offered some alternative ideas and perspectives for treatment and medications. Ultimately, however, we hit a wall there, too. We became overwhelmed with constantly driving to her practice, located in Kentucky, and struggling to keep Skyler occupied during our lengthy wait for his scheduled appointments when she was behind.

Just when I thought we had seen and/or tried it all, an acquaintance in the autism community forwarded me a clinical article written by a physician from New York. He utilized his experience with Transcranial Direct Current Stimulation (TDCS), which uses a neuromodulating device that delivers a very weak, imperceptible electric current to the brain via a battery-powered pack to re-stimulate damaged brain tissue with patients who have suffered from a range of medical conditions. He applied the research with TDCS to those on the autism spectrum and suggested that neuromodulation,

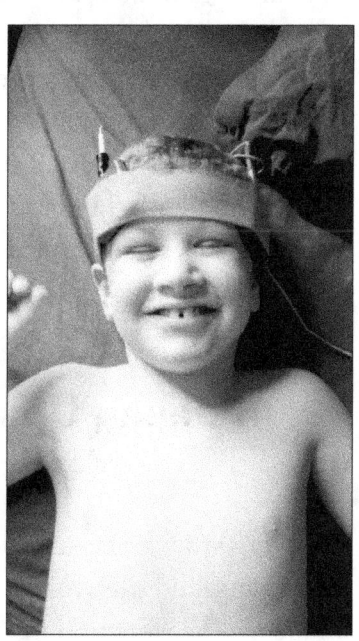

Skyler, all hooked up for one of his TDCS treatments

when applied to the dysfunctional areas of the brain associated with language, could be successful in combating language deficits. I reviewed his background and promising research and — because this treatment would not inflict pain or harm to Skyler — it seemed definitely worth pursuing.

Before I could wrap my head around flying with eight-year-old Skyler to New York each month for this radical treatment (which was not likely feasible), I learned that a local autism mom had secured funding and made arrangements for this physician to travel to our small community in Indiana to conduct patient interactions locally. It seemed like, once again, God stepped in to provide Skyler with every opportunity imaginable! Equally as amazing, the office space utilized for the TDCS therapy sessions was located five minutes from my house.

As with every treatment before, it was given a two-year trial window by my ex-husband, who demanded evidence of miraculous transformations if he was going to continue paying his share of the treatment. Like most autism treatments, TDCS was deemed "experimental" by the insurance company and, thus, we paid completely out of pocket. Sadly, Skyler hadn't uttered a single word or sound throughout the two years so, yet again, my hopes for speech were dashed, and our visits with Dr. New York came to an end.

Feeling Unwelcome, Even in the Medical Community

For the next several years, we took a break from chasing novel treatments, and tried to resolve Skyler's behaviors strictly with medicine. We were hoping ABA and speech therapies would be the turning point, but nothing clicked. I made a PECS book for my house (a special tool using what's called the Picture Exchange Communication System, for communicating with nonverbal children) and I tried to get my ex-husband to use one too, though he refused. I was hoping to establish some communication for Skyler, but without the consistency of both homes doing the same thing, nothing resonated with him. We also tried extensive potty-training methods. At this time, Skyler's biological father had joint custody and his refusal to cooperate with any of these efforts made them doomed to fail, as I only physically had contact with Skyler for two weeks out of each month.

While we were on our break from any new, revolutionary therapies, I revisited our need for a local pediatrician. Luckily, Skyler infrequently suffers from the flu, GI bug or other seasonal illnesses, but I didn't want to press our luck. Per several recommendations, I found a pediatrician closer to home who was also very supportive with trying alternative treatments for patients like Skyler. Our new doctor was thorough from the very first office visit, asking lots of questions about what we've tried over the years regarding medication and therapies and also which specialists we've been to and what tests had been completed.

During Skyler's age-14 wellness visit, the doctor suggested that, although Skyler's hearing tests (performed years earlier) proved normal, the extensive amounts of brownish-red wax in his ears (which we clean daily during his bath, but it keeps coming back) could be causing an issue. The pediatrician thought we should have an ear/nose/throat doctor (ENT) look at Skyler and flush his ear canal to remove excess wax buildup. Sounds easy enough, right?

Wrong.

Skyler's doctor referred us to a large ENT group, and when I called to schedule the appointment, I was assured that the group had experience with potentially uncooperative special-needs patients. When I say it was the absolute worst experience in all my years of parenting, even that feels like an understatement. Of course, Skyler can be difficult to manage at any appointment, but I have it down to a science when it comes to how to hold him, how to block him from throwing things or smacking innocent people, and how to proactively anticipate his quick movements. On this day, as I was trying to sign his name on the clipboard at the reception desk, Skyler quickly reached for the cup of pens, the Kleenex box and anything else on the counter he could throw, but I managed to thwart his efforts with my other hand. We paced the waiting room, and I stayed my usual one step ahead of him, predicting his every move. Practically sweating through my clothes from all the activity, I glanced over to the desk to check the clock and caught a glimpse of the receptionist watching us with wide eyes. She shouted through the glass window between us, "Wow, you are amazing with him!" I smiled.

> **Skyler can be difficult to manage at any appointment, but I have it down to a science when it comes to how to hold him, how to block him from throwing things or smacking innocent people, and how to proactively anticipate his quick movements.**

We were taken back to the exam room, and the nurse collected some general information from us. She was very kind and politely smiled and sloughed off Skyler's attempts to take the file and pen from her while she was writing. Moments later, the physician walked into the room, and Skyler instinctively smacked him on the arm, which is not uncommon (given his past experiences) when he's nervous and uncertain about what a man in a white coat is going to do to him. I apologized profusely and the physician stepped up to Skyler's face and, with furrowed brows and a scowl, loudly proclaimed, "Whoa! Don't you do that again!" I was shocked. For a minute, I thought he was joking around. Did he really just yell at my child?

Thankfully, Skyler didn't seem affected in the slightest. He carried on his attempts to touch everything in sight, while the hostility in the exam room grew palpable. The physician then asked me why we were there, to which I softly responded, "To flush his ears because of impacted wax." The banter between the doctor and me was brief but seemingly strained from his end. He asked how in the world he was supposed to examine Skyler's ears, let alone flush them, with him hitting people because "We won't tolerate that behavior."

Still somehow maintaining my composure, I apologized and explained that I always hold Skyler in my lap while other doctors have evaluated him and it works out just fine. The physician looked me square in the eyes, clearly irritated, and scolded me that due to Skyler's "violence," he would need to be sedated for the procedure, which they can't do in the office, so it's probably best to just leave the wax in there and schedule an appointment with the surgery center (which this doctor also owns) for sedation.

I felt like I was in the Twilight Zone! Stunned by being essentially asked to leave, I could feel my face redden as my blood boiled, and my eyes began filling with tears. I quickly gathered my things and ushered Skyler out to the waiting room. With one foot into the waiting room, the physician stopped me to make an insincere attempt to appear understanding of the situation. I know he was putting on a show to save face in front of the staff, who could clearly see how upset I was. He blurted out, "Well I don't want to make you upset but we just can't help you here."

I had completely come unhinged by this point and told him that I was very clear when scheduling the appointment that my son has autism and is non-verbal, and the scheduler told me that would not be a problem. Having to get the last word, the physician retorted with, "Schedulers aren't doctors." I wanted to say, "But given your bedside manner, not all doctors are professional," but I swallowed my words to get the hell out of there.

Mind you, I'm no stranger to interacting with physicians. I work in pharmaceutical sales. As such, my career for the past 20 years has involved daily conversations and interactions with physicians of varying specialties and personalities. But never in my life had I met a medical professional so ignorant or cruel — so utterly lacking compassion for the patient or the circumstance — until that day.

Never in my life had I met a medical professional so ignorant or cruel — so utterly lacking compassion for the patient or the circumstance — until that day.

I held it together long enough to drop Skyler off at his autism center. I didn't want him to see me upset. By this point in our lives, I was no longer parenting the kids alone but was happily married to Josh, who was always in my corner and could always help me through my darkest moments. I called Josh the moment I got back to my car and bawled uncontrollably. To witness my child being disrespected and tossed aside made me so incredibly angry. I couldn't help but envision his life as an adult. How frequently will similar situations of ignorance happen to him and what will he do when I'm no longer there to protect him?

Big Progress, Major Explorations

As he settled into his teen years, Skyler's mildly aggressive behaviors didn't seem to be improving with any consistency, and he had been on the same medications for several years. So we felt it was time to find another psychiatry group to assist us. Josh suggested that we take Skyler to see Carrie Schanie, a psychiatric nurse practitioner (NP) who was a close friend and who also had extensive experience with people on the spectrum. She had participated in several clinical trials regarding medication treatments for autism. Thankfully, despite her full patient load, she accepted Skyler as a patient. She was extremely thorough and strategic with her analysis of past medicines we'd tried (and the resulting behaviors) before deciding to make some drastic and necessary improvements to his medications. She absolutely loves her job and shows great passion for helping her patients live a better quality of life. Skyler's overall behavior has dramatically improved with the changes she implemented, and we could not be more pleased!

Identifying medications that help calm Skyler's stimming (i.e., self-stimulatory behaviors like clapping overhead or swiping the side of his cheek with his hand repeatedly) and his aggressiveness is only one piece of his behavior puzzle. A topic Josh and I routinely revisit with every medical professional we meet is how Skyler's digestion appears to be causing him extreme discomfort. Throughout most of his lifetime, Skyler has been consistently constipated for five to six days in row. The open-handed banging on walls, countertops and himself, and the hitting of other people was off the charts in frequency and seemed to ramp up as the consecutive days of constipation increased. In the past, we were advised to give him apple juice, stool softeners and lots and lots of MiraLAX.

In addition to the constipation, Skyler developed a tendency several years ago to "choke" frequently when eating. We often chalked it up to us feeding him bites that were too large for his throat or the fact that he was always so excited to eat that he was terrible at chewing and preferred to inhale his food. The pediatrician was very concerned with all of Skyler's digestive issues, most dire being the choking, so he referred us to a feeding clinic where nutritionists and dietitians could observe Skyler eating. We were also sent to the local children's hospital, where X-rays and barium swallow studies were completed.

The barium swallow test requires the patient to swallow barium sulfate either by drinking it or eating it. The barium is a thick, white, milky substance that frankly tastes like metallic glue. An X-ray is taken as the barium sulfate is consumed so abnormalities in the esophagus and stomach or issues with chewing and swallowing can be quickly identified. Skyler was a champ, downing several gulps of the mixture while strapped to the seated X-ray machine, with Josh and me flanked on both sides, one feeding him and the other holding him still.

The radiologist was unable to identify any abnormalities with his esophagus nor issues with his swallowing. So, aside from telling us to be sure we provided him very small portions when feeding tough-to-chew food (e.g., chicken, bread, pasta), the secondary suggestion from the nutrition clinic was that we consider giving him an all-liquid diet. Sure, that's reasonable for a 15-year-old who *loves* food! My mom-warrior intuition told me they were missing something; choking on practically every meal during the past six months, and five consecutive days of constipation each week cannot be normal.

The pediatrician agreed that we needed to press further so he next sent us to the University of Louisville Pediatric Gastroenterology office. I recounted practically every detail of Skyler's 15-year history of gastroenterological (GI) issues to the NP but felt like I was not being heard. I explained the constipation, banging, choking, etc., and inquired about whether a colonoscopy would reveal a clearer picture of what may be going on. She told me she was more concerned with the choking than the constipation and said what he really needed was an endoscopy. Although I still felt she was missing the bigger picture and was wrong for dismissing the idea of a colonoscopy, I scheduled the endoscopy. In the meantime, she advised that we double the amount of MiraLAX we were giving Skyler to help the constipation. I left the doctor's office feeling frustrated, and we feared we were failing this poor voiceless, suffering kid. I prayed and prayed for guidance and ideas about what to do next.

We feared we were failing this poor voiceless, suffering kid. I prayed and prayed for guidance and ideas about what to do next.

A few days after the appointment, I recalled a conversation I'd had with a close friend about her young son on the spectrum who also suffers greatly from constipation and feeding issues. She had taken her son out of state to see a pediatric GI specialist who works exclusively with patients on the autism spectrum. I called her, and the similarities between her son's behaviors and Skyler's were eerily similar as it related to digestion issues. She encouraged me to reach out to their doctor's office and get some additional information. That was one of the best calls I've ever made on Skyler's behalf.

We got on the doctor's schedule rather quickly and had our first appointment with the specialist via Skype because he was based in New York. I was surprised and unsure what to think when I watched him continuously nodding and smiling while we relayed Skyler's medical history. He later told us that Skyler's symptoms mirrored 90% of the patients he treated. He was confident he could help us and explained the process and procedures in detail. We opted to travel to Austin, Texas, (where he also conducts office visits and procedures one week each month) for Skyler's treatment instead of New York. I was a nervous wreck from the minute the flights were booked. Skyler had only flown once before (a few months earlier) and did quite well, but he is a bit of a wild card, so we never know what to expect.

After a very uneventful flight to Austin (thank you, Jesus), we got checked into our hotel room. Now, a check-in to a hotel for us is not like a check-in for most people. The first thing Josh and I must do is rearrange the furniture to ensure Skyler will not be in a position to wander around the room all night. At home, he is used to sleeping on a mattress on the floor surrounded by lots of body pillows in an enclosed space, so we must recreate that environment as best as we can in a hotel room.

As such, we always request the largest room available, which often comes with a couch. We pull the couch away from the wall and place a mattress (from the roll-away bed that we ask for in advance) on the floor behind the couch and up against the wall. The other sides of the "boxed-in fort" we build him consist of tables, chairs, couch cushions, etc. Of course, while Josh dismantles the hotel room, I am usually passing the time by walking Skyler through the halls of the hotel or lapping the building outside until the construction of our son's personalized space is completed. Regardless of our attempts to give Skyler a somewhat comfortable and safe place to sleep, he does not sleep well in an unfamiliar environment, so as predicted, this particular night in Austin, he ended up staying awake all night, which meant we did, too.

We arrived, exhausted, at the physician's office the next morning, and again I prayed hard that Skyler would be a cooperative patient and swallow the *very* large, *very* expensive pill camera, which was a crucial step in the evaluation. Skyler at first kept spitting it out and refused to swallow it. I was beyond stressed and impatient, so I left the room with the nurse to discuss alternatives if he was unable to swallow the pill. Meanwhile, Josh much more calmly worked with Skyler. Moments later, Josh walked into the nurse's office and nonchalantly said, "He swallowed it. We're good." I should have known; Josh always works his magic as the "Skyler whisperer" and can get that kid to do anything!

Skyler was a champ wearing the belt (which housed the power box and recorder for the pill camera) for a solid eight hours without a single hassle. (I like to think our genius idea of putting him in a backward Elmo onesie significantly helped keep his hands from touching the fanny pack where the recorder was housed.) We passed much of the time driving around exploring Austin, taking walks outside around the hotel (during which we received lots of staring due to Skyler's cut-off Elmo onesie — worn backward) and watching Elmo movies via YouTube from our cell phones.

His endoscopy and colonoscopy were scheduled for the following afternoon, so next on the agenda was Skyler's colon prep (i.e., bowel cleanout). If you think this is a complicated and unpleasant process for an able-bodied adult,

Skyler lapping the hotel in Austin, in his Elmo onesie, backwards

imagine it for a severely autistic teenager who is not potty-trained. Trying to tag-team his pull-up changes in a tiny hotel bathroom presented an entirely new set of challenges. We made it through mostly unscathed and due to the prior two days of fasting and cleanout, he actually slept like a baby that night, meaning we were able to finally rest, too!

Once the procedures were finished, and we waited for Skyler to wake from sedation, the physician reported that his predictions were correct, and Skyler's intestines and insides were much worse than he thought. He explained that, for the bulk of his life, Skyler had been suffering greatly from ulcerative colitis (an inflammatory bowel disease that results in inflammation and ulcers in the colon and rectum), as well as esophageal disease. He shared the upper and lower scope images with us and pointed out the vast number of ulcers stretching from Skyler's throat down to his rectum, most of which also coated most of his intestines. My eyes filled with tears and I hugged the doctor while thanking him profusely for taking us seriously. I expressed my gratitude for his willingness to devote his practice to evaluating, diagnosing and treating kids with co-morbidities to autism when no one seems to take warrior moms like me seriously.

Josh and I were emotionally overwhelmed as we thought about the amount of pain Skyler had been in for years. It finally explained so clearly the reasoning for his incessant banging and self-injury, as well as the all-too-frequent constipation and choking. Having all of this information and a true diagnosis answered my prayers, but now what? Could this suffering and pain be fixed?

Having all of this information and a true diagnosis answered my prayers, but now what? Could this suffering and pain be fixed?

We headed back to the airport, armed with a handful of prescriptions and a plan that we prayed would immediately start healing our boy's GI tract. Skyler's treatment protocol began with several months of steroids, an anti-inflammatory agent that helps control the stomach pain and side effects of colitis, and an antibiotic that targets and treats bacteria in the stomach and intestinal tract. Thankfully, Skyler responded well to those treatments and we identified a noticeable decrease in the banging and negative behaviors, while at the same time witnessed his bowel movements normalize. After many months on these medications, his beautiful smile also returned and his focus and attention gradually improved.

Needles and Complications

The next step in the healing process required us to administer a bi-monthly injection of a biologic agent into Skyler's thigh, which would help control the inflammation and pain caused by the ulcerative colitis. The physician advised that we should begin seeing positive effects from the treatment by the fifth injection. With each injection beyond the fifth, our hopes were dashed. The symptom relief was non-existent, his negative behaviors returned with a vengeance and, even worse, we noticed some really horrific ailments randomly attacking his body — making life even more challenging for all of us.

Skyler has always had severely cracked heels, requiring prescription ointments and creams from both dermatologists and podiatrists. However, prior to starting all the GI treatments, the many months of daily lathering of ointments had done the trick and "healed the heels," as we say. Once the steroids were discontinued and the injectable medication began, we observed Skyler's feet literally go from normal to split open overnight. When the previous treatments no longer worked, we slathered lanolin mixed with some essential oils onto his feet, and wrapped them with cling wrap before placing his socks on. No

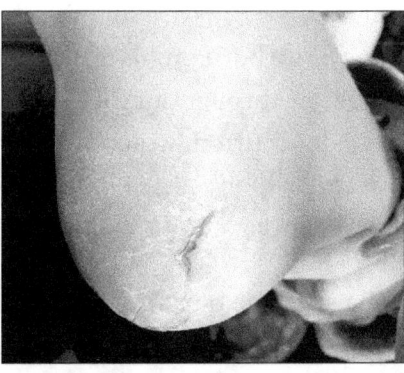

Skyler's heel and foot fissures

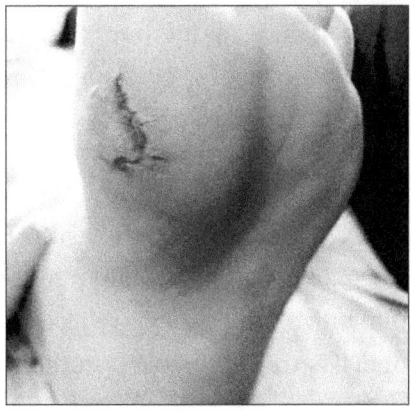

matter what we tried, it seemed the fissures were beyond repair. Skyler began toe walking and limping, which he has never in his life done before, to avoid the surge of pain when placing his heels on the floor. It was heartbreaking.

In addition to the fissures, we began noticing what we thought were random pimples developing all over his body. One would appear on his right thigh then another on his upper left arm. A few sprouted up on his buttocks then one on his neck. We treated the spots with some acne creams and didn't think much of it until they no longer presented as garden-variety pimples but became scabbed over, eventually leaving a scar to permanently record where the sore had been. This continued on for several months until, one evening during his bath, we caught a glimpse of a clustering of spots resembling a rug burn on his left elbow. Assuming that he likely injured his elbow throughout the day and didn't acknowledge or react when it occurred, which is typical for a non-verbal child with an extremely high pain tolerance, I coated the sores with Neosporin and a bandage.

We awoke the next morning to find Skyler's elbow swollen and each sore oozing with puss. It appeared he was unable to straighten and extend his arm without wincing. Josh and I glanced at each other and, without the need to say more than "let's go to the ED," we got dressed and steered our car to the Children's Hospital. I honestly think parents of special-needs children should get a punch card and after 10 punches, the 11th visit is no charge!

The Emergency Department physician could not have been nicer. We provided all the background we could think of about the various sores and medication changes over the past few months and, to maximize our co-pay, we asked if she could also take a look at his heel fissures as well. As predicted, we were advised to continue

Neosporin on both his feet and random sores and were given yet another antibiotic.

Throughout these months of puzzling ailments, I expressed concern based on my mother's intuition to our GI physician that the timing of these issues seemed to coincide with starting the bi-monthly biologic injection. He assured me that the injection likely didn't cause the side effects that Skyler was experiencing and, having researched the medication package insert thoroughly beforehand, I couldn't disagree with him. However, it didn't make me feel any better and I couldn't escape the nagging feeling that we were perhaps making Skyler feel worse instead of better.

At this point, Skyler had received his sixth injection and there were absolutely no benefits observed. He was regressing, terribly. Not only was his body outwardly suffering, but I envisioned his GI tract was unbearably painful as well because his banging, hitting and raging was at an all-time high.

Those last few months we continued the injections I spent wrestling with my internal dialogue — *"Maybe the next shot will be the one he needs before we begin noticing positive changes. But if we keep waiting to see if it helps, are we causing the poor kid more suffering?"* Being a mom is just frickin' hard in general, but it really sucks when your child has an illness that you can't see and they can't tell you where it hurts.

Being a mom is just frickin' hard in general, but it really sucks when your child has an illness that you can't see and they can't tell you where it hurts.

More Suffering Than We Could Bear

The nagging hope in the back of my mind of helping treat Skyler's ulcerative colitis moved to the forefront and, as such, stifled my gut instinct of stopping the medication. We proceeded with injection seven and eight. Again, nothing but turmoil. The eighth injection would be our last.

The final straw for us came with a phone call from Skyler's ABA Center. The voice of the RBT (registered behavioral technician) on the other end of the line was shaking when he mentioned that, while changing Skyler's pull-up, there was a noticeable amount of blood and his scrotum was severely inflamed. I gasped and my eyes welled with tears. This resilient and tough-as-nails kid can't catch a damn break! I called our pediatrician, who instructed this was far beyond any diaper rash and he prescribed a three-step cream application (i.e., three different creams and ointments to be applied in a specific sequence) that must be done after each pull-up change. The ABA Center happily obliged adding this to Skyler's daily routine.

Within a few weeks, we would be traveling to New York for our annual follow-up appointment with Skyler's GI doctor. Through emails and Skype calls, we had been keeping him up to date with the issues — the skin sores, the cracked heels and now the inflamed scrotum. I must say that, although the doctor wasn't quick to discontinue the medication early on, he agreed with me that something was very wrong and we halted the injections after number eight. Several labs, stool samples, and X-rays were ordered to try to determine why Skyler's system was rejecting various forms of treatment.

Thankfully, due to unseasonably sunny skies for the East Coast in January and a practically empty plane, our flight to New York was uneventful. While our appointment provided clarity about some things, it unfortunately generated additional unanswered questions.

The physician explained that the "random skin sores" were actually abscesses and the inflammation of Skyler's scrotum was a severe fungal infection. He elaborated further that my gut instinct was correct. Skyler's immune system became compromised from the injectable that was supposed to be healing him. Ultimately, it provided no medical benefit for Skyler, only terrible side effects.

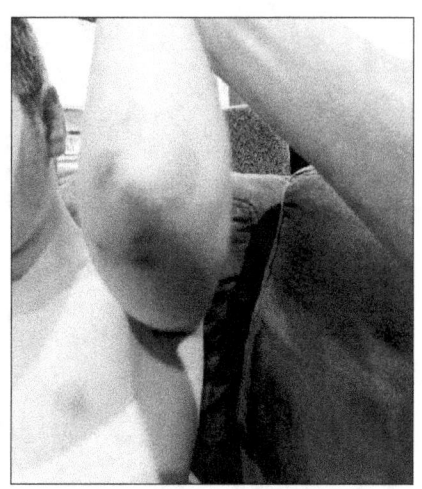

Abscesses on Skyler's elbow

Like before, we flew home with a revised plan for healing and the assurance from Skyler's physician that, believe it or not, our boy is not the most challenging autistic patient in his practice.

This is the most difficult part about having a non-verbal child. He can't communicate that his intestines twist into knots every time he experiences extreme gas cramps or that the passing of poop is so painful that he panics and distracts himself by banging walls. Those aren't things we can see. It's beyond heartbreaking to watch your child suffer, knowing you are unable to take their pain away to make it your own. So, we continue to track behaviors and visit one doctor after another until we unlock some answers. Unfortunately, this process may take years or even a lifetime. For us, it has been a never-ending battle.

It's beyond heartbreaking to watch your child suffer, knowing you are unable to take their pain away to make it your own. So, we continue to track behaviors and visit one doctor after another until we unlock some answers

CHAPTER SIX

The Effects of Autism on Sibling Relationships

Skyler was almost two years old when my then-husband and
I discovered we were pregnant with our daughter, Kendall. I vividly
remember the entire 38-week pregnancy; I was a nervous wreck.
For the entire nine months, I ate an incredibly healthy diet, and
I meticulously monitored everything and everyone I came in contact
with. While I was beyond excited to bring another beautiful child
into the world, I was overwhelmed with fear that she would have
health challenges or special needs, which seemed more than I could
possibly handle. *What was the medical probability of having two children with autism,* I wondered?

On the day of Kendall's arrival, my anxiety reached a fever pitch.
I had a full-blown panic attack and required oxygen during

Kendall's delivery. I couldn't shake my legitimate concerns that if something was wrong, it would be more than I could bear. How would I have the time and energy to devote to another child in need of therapies and medical intervention on a daily basis? All my fears had been for nothing; we welcomed a healthy baby girl. The doctor repeatedly assured me that Kendall was fine — healthy, without complications or handicaps or birth defects. It was a huge relief. But I was still worried, and I was destined to worry for years. You see, Kendall's healthy exterior didn't stop me from feverishly tracking her every developmental milestone, nearly all of which she conquered earlier than expected.

I had a full-blown panic attack and required oxygen during Kendall's delivery. I couldn't shake my legitimate concerns that if something was wrong, it would be more than I could bear. How would I have the time and energy to devote to another child in need of therapies and medical intervention on a daily basis?

Kendall was a gorgeous baby who was quite smart and quickly learned to never take her eyes off her curious brother. He, however, showed zero interest in the squawking baby who rested comfortably nearby in her Pack and Play portable crib. Skyler couldn't have cared less that she could feed herself, crawl, walk and babble. He remained in his own private world, oblivious to those around him.

While I was elated that Kendall's development was cognitively and socially on track, it only accentuated for me how autism had robbed Skyler of these same accomplishments. It was a strange phenomenon knowing that this should be the *second* time I'm witnessing all of these treasured moments, not the first.

While I was elated that Kendall's development was cognitively and socially on track, it only accentuated for me how autism had robbed Skyler of these same accomplishments.

I distinctly recall the first time Kendall looked me very purposefully in the eyes and said "momma." I bawled ugly, grateful, elated but heartbroken tears. My crying frightened her and she started crying in return. I felt so badly, but my reaction was sincerely one of amazement and pride because, until that moment, I had never before been called "Mom" by either of my children. It was surreal.

Growing Up with a Special Brother Made Kendall a Special Sister

In a world in which siblings are typically our first playmates and our best friends, Kendall was destined for a different childhood from what most kids experience. She had a brother, but she was, in many ways, alone. I remember watching over my kids and thinking about how their experiences and their relationship dynamic was so different from what I'd always known (and hoped for when it came to my own children). Reflecting on my own childhood experiences and memories with a sibling just 17 months older than me, I recalled following my older sister like her shadow, mimicking her every move and soaking up all she would teach me. We spent countless hours every day making forts, playing games or riding our bikes around the neighborhood, scouting out new opportunities to get ourselves in trouble. Even as we aged and our relationship went from unicorns and rainbows to teenage bickering about who borrowed clothes from whom without asking first, we always found our way back to being each other's biggest supporter and protector. So, watching Kendall evolve independently from an energetic, chatty and silly little sister into a high schooler preparing for college and her future — while her brother, although age 17 at the time of this book's release remains in the development of a toddler — troubles me greatly. Kendall is moving forward and, for Skyler, time stands still.

Someday, Kendall might have children of her own, and I wonder about the stories she'll tell them about her own childhood. It saddens me to think that she won't have similar memories of childhood shenanigans with her brother, like the stories I tell about my sister. I realize our experiences are uniquely beautiful, but I can't help but focus on what she's missed.

As much as I try to put myself in Kendall's shoes, I struggle to fully comprehend what it must be like having a sibling you cannot communicate with, play with or relate to in any way. I imagine it must be confusing and sad to never know where she fits into his world — to not know what he

Skyler and Kendall in 2006

thinks of her or feels for her, and to wonder about whether the role she was born into as unofficial sibling caregiver is a responsibility she can handle as time goes by. Kendall and Skyler unconsciously switched roles many years ago, with the younger sister assuming the role of teacher and caregiver for her "older little brother.'"

Beginning when the kids were young, I focused heavily on treating them exactly the same and encouraged Kendall to find a way to include Skyler when she played. To this day, it melts my heart to look back at pictures and videos of them "playing" together, which usually amounted to her reluctantly fetching his chewy tube and other sensory mouthing toys that were covered in spit every time he threw them. Personally, I think he was smart enough to figure out that this little sister who had arrived in his world could be quite useful to him!

It was always "monkey see, monkey do" between them, but it was the opposite of how it should be, as Kendall was always teaching Skyler something new. Kendall walked first, clearly talked first (and has *never* stopped since! Ha!), and introduced Skyler to the songs and cartoons he continues to love. While she seemed to easily

Kendall being a "big little sister," playing with her brother in 2007

adapt to her brother's abilities when attempting to play and follow him, we all learned a hard lesson that Skyler had no comprehension of boundaries or the pain he could inflict on his sweet, defenseless sister.

Kendall and Skyler going on a wagon ride in 2007

When he was about three and his little sister Kendall was just learning to crawl and walk, Skyler developed a fetish for hair, thread and string. After a blood-curdling shriek, a "No Syla!" scream and a river of little-girl tears, I quickly discovered that I could not leave both kids alone playing in the same room for even a minute because Skyler would literally rip a handful of hair from Kendall's head. Sometimes, it was almost as if he was wise enough to patiently wait until she was backed into a corner of the room playing then make his move, grab a section of her hair, then silently crawl away as she wailed. The hair pulling was clearly an odd sensory input he needed to fulfill because, though he never actually ate hair or thread, he liked drawing it across his lips repeatedly (like a bow across a violin's strings) as if the texture of it was soothing to him.

From the moment Skyler pulled his sister's hair for the first time, I tried every creative solution I could think of to save her precious locks of hair and keep her from suffering at the hands of her brother. I first bought him a Bratz doll styling head, so he would go after the long locks of doll hair and not Kendall's. When that didn't work, I carried around a spool of thread and a container of dental floss. If I saw him make a move toward his sister, I tore off a piece of floss or thread and handed it to him. This went on for years until Kendall learned to keep her head on a swivel and always be looking over her shoulder, which broke my heart. No child should have to be fearful of her own sibling, but here we were ... living that very scenario.

> **No child should have to be fearful
> of her own sibling, but here we were
> ... living that very scenario.**

The beauty behind the innocence of young children is that they quickly forgive and forget. By nature, they also tend to be very accepting when recognizing the differences in others and certainly don't see those differences as a hindrance to playing with them. When Kendall was about five years old and could better understand some of the social challenges and developmental delays Skyler experienced, she voluntarily assumed the role of protector and supporter of her brother, even though I have tried desperately to remind her that she is not responsible for anything other than enjoying being a kid.

One of her frequent games with Skyler involved a sensory room in our home that we filled wall to wall with plastic balls. (It became a dedicated sensory "ball pit room" after we learned that Skyler was fearful of getting into the actual ball-pit structure we had bought him but that he *loved* sitting in and wading through huge piles of colored balls. No problem! Ditch the structure and fill the entire room with balls!) In her typical, thoughtful fashion, Kendall spent hours desperately trying to teach him colors by yelling out, "Skyler, throw the red ball" or "Throw the green ball" to no avail. He just enjoyed throwing any ball near him, which sent her fetching those plastic balls over and over, sometimes for an hour or more at a time.

At one of her first birthday sleepovers, around age eight or nine, Kendall innocently announced to each girl as they arrived to our home: "You probably want to stay away from my brother because he has 'the autism' and he likes to pull hair." I was mortified and also laughing hysterically at the same time. None of the little girls with beautiful, long hair were fazed by Kendall's warning and all said hello to Skyler as they skipped past. Josh wanted to make light of the situation and, let's be honest, he enjoys making kids laugh by acting like a big kid himself, so he scooped up Skyler and ran around the house chasing all the little girls. The kids squealed, giggled and Skyler laughed so hard he cried. All the girls had fun, Kendall didn't feel embarrassed or awkward (well, maybe by goofy Josh), and Skyler was semi-included in the weekend's festivities ... so it was a successful sleepover. I probably should've enjoyed that "mom win" moment a bit longer because the "parenting failures" to come would certainly dwindle my confidence in having this whole autism crap figured out!

Holiday Traditions and Festive Celebrations (Sort of)

Over the years, we've learned to navigate through birthday parties and celebrations for both kids in sincere hopes of ensuring they know how special the day of their birth is to us. Kendall has had many over-the-top themed parties where she was the center of attention and could escape the stigma of having a special-needs sibling for an entire day. In some ways, birthdays are easy … but other holidays and significant events always present a challenge. We always wonder, *"How can we adapt our plans so Kendall has a good time and Skyler isn't left out of the fun?"*

I could honestly scroll down the list of major holidays where family traditions are developed when children are very young. Take Easter, for example. Skyler has never been able to participate in Easter egg hunts, has no comprehension of the excitement that should come from seeing the loot left by the Easter bunny and struggles to tolerate "church clothes" let alone sit through the lengthy Easter mass. So, trying to be mother extraordinaire, I tasked myself with dragging Skyler along to all these events so Kendall wouldn't miss out and, despite Skyler hating candy and chocolate of any kind, I ensured that the Easter bunny always filled their baskets with identical treats and gifts.

Halloween presents similar challenges. During the early years, when both kids would fit in a double seated wagon, I was able to buckle Skyler in and let Kendall hop out to trick-or-treat. When she would ask if Skyler wanted to go up to the houses with her, I would just provide the excuse that he was tired and couldn't eat much candy because of his special diet, so we would happily wait for her. As they grew too large for wagons and we didn't yet own a suitable stroller for Skyler, I would attempt to hold his hand and walk him around the

Kendall, Halloween 2009

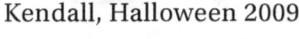

Laurie and her Very
Hungry Caterpillar, Skyler
– Halloween 2010

neighborhood. It never failed that he would walk for only the first five minutes then insist on being carried — and he was not exactly light at the ages of seven to ten! Kendall — being the sweet, thoughtful and empathetic little sister that she is — decided to carry Skyler's treat bag on her other arm so that she could trick-or-treat for him. She hated the thought of him being left out of the fun. It was heart-rending but also made me incredibly proud. Here was this tiny, little girl dragging two bags, ringing the doorbells of strangers and confidently explaining the situation of the extra bag on her arm while pointing to her brother, propped up on my hip.

Next comes Thanksgiving, where the thought of attending a formal meal with fine china and fancy decorations at any home other than ours gives me anxiety. Frankly, I feel the same anxiety when faced with all the invitations to Christmas parties throughout much of December. The destruction Skyler is capable of simply by having curious hands in an unfamiliar environment turns into overwhelming embarrassment for all of us, but as a child still trying to process her feelings, sadly, Kendall becomes the most affected. While she's used to unwrapping all her brother's gifts for him (because he honestly couldn't care less about presents) and she's well aware that we will be feeding him at the dinner table (where everyone will watch and stare), I am certain she's tired of the spectacle that is autism.

My biggest concern is Kendall coming to me — years from now, maybe after she's become a mother — to express her feelings that her brother and his autism ruined her childhood memories and any chance of developing family traditions to share with her children. And, if I'm being honest, I worry that she'll blame me for not trying harder to give her more of a normal life. But perhaps

Skyler and Kendall in 2015

I'm underestimating her as a "warrior sister" and diminishing my own impact as a strong and loving mother. I hope Kendall recognizes that she's been provided a different set of tools in her toolbox to tackle the unique challenges parenthood may bring her one day. She might be more patient, more understanding, more flexible, more spontaneous, more giving, more forgiving, more accepting and more loving ... because of autism, not in spite of it.

A Complicated and Special Relationship

Just like with my sister (and probably most siblings), the relationship between Skyler and Kendall frequently goes through cycles of love for each other followed by despising one another the very next week. As they've become teenagers, Skyler continues to annoy Kendall non-stop because he's more aware of the attention she gets from us, which is far too much for his liking. One of Skyler's favorite ways to annoy Kendall currently is to take the pencil right from her hand as she's doing homework. He also occasionally catches her off guard when she's sitting on the couch and does what we call a "drive-by." For no apparent reason, he will walk behind the couch and pull out a handful of her hair, which is obviously quite painful and traumatizing to Kendall, seeing as he's done that to her all her life. She hollers "I hate you!" and "Why can't you just be normal?!" ... to which I just hang my head and feel completely defeated. Kendall's angry with me because I don't "punish" him; I'm angry with Skyler because he can't keep his hands to himself; and, all the while, Skyler wanders toward the television to watch Sesame Street, completely oblivious to the chaos he just created. His actions, good or bad, clearly set the tone and mood of the entire household.

**His actions, good or bad, clearly set the
tone and mood of the entire household.**

Skyler is a professional pest with incredible stamina for repeating naughty behavior for hours. Kendall is an avid baker and also loves helping me create new gluten-free meal ideas for Skyler. However, unless we barricade ourselves in the kitchen with barstools when we're cooking together, Skyler will insist on "helping" and, well, we don't consider throwing all our ingredients and utensils to the floor to be that much help. Josh always saves the day by taking Skyler for a walk or to a different room until we are finished. Despite being annoyed, I do find it adorable that every time Josh removes Skyler from the kitchen, he asks him: "Are you being a helper or a hurter?" ... to which Skyler always giggles and smiles. He's very intelligent and knows exactly what buttons to push with all of us. He's used to one-to-one attention from 8:00 a.m. to 4:00 p.m. five days a week at his Autism Center so, in his opinion, he should also be the sole focus of every moment spent at home.

On the flip side, Kendall has a tendency to pace around our living room couch (she says it settles her anxiety) which irritates her brother because he is trying to watch one of his multiple "Elmo's World" DVDs, and she's walking in front of the television. The irony is lost on him that he does the exact same thing when the rest of us try to watch anything other than Elmo. (Kendall constantly

Skyler and Kendall in 2017

hurls "You make a better door than a window" in his direction.) He waits for her to pass by and takes off chasing after her. She screams while laughing and yells for help from Mom or Josh, which we ignore. Both of them drive us crazy with the ridiculously high-decibel level of our house, but we wouldn't change a thing. If the only interactions they have with one another are foot chases around the furniture and smacks on the arm, I'll take it. All too soon, Kendall will be off to college, and our home will seem eerily quiet, so we choose to savor the chaos! Not to mention that we have purposefully created an environment of interaction, rather than isolating Skyler from the rest of the family. This is as "normal" an upbringing for Skyler and Kendall to grow up together as possible. It's just a shame it only happens every other week, because Kendall spends half her time with her biological dad.

As the kids get older, we find ourselves a household with two teenagers who look similar in age but whose behaviors and needs couldn't be further apart. Kendall lives like a teenager and Skyler still behaves like a little boy. Some days, it's sad for us all to observe and process. So, I try to focus on the silver linings. For us, there will be no complaining from Kendall about having to share a bathroom with a sibling who takes excessively long showers. There will be no fights over who has priority over taking the car. There will be no arguments in the morning to hurry up or they'll be late for school. There will be no negotiations about trading chores.

As Kendall grows up and ages into new experiences, I again revisit the worries I had when the kids were little. I regularly ask myself questions about what she may be thinking or feeling; not having a typical older sibling to pave the way for her has left her lonely but not alone. Does it sadden her that she will never get the "big brother guidance," dating advice or social benefits that come from having a sibling two years ahead of you in school? I remember that when I took her to freshman orientation for high school, I couldn't help but feel a bit sad that Skyler wasn't able to prepare her for all things high school: offering insider information about the best teachers to get, giving her a tour of the school, or providing her with the feeling of protection that comes with having a big brother who is an upper-classman. It's in those moments that I daydream about what this exact situation looks and sounds like in the homes of my friends with daughters and sons the same ages as mine. The constant ribbing and teasing between siblings that probably annoys most parents actually sounds like a piece of heaven to me.

> **I daydream about what this exact situation looks and sounds like in the homes of my friends with daughters and sons the same ages as mine. The constant ribbing and teasing between siblings that probably annoys most parents actually sounds like a piece of heaven to me.**

After Josh's adoption of Skyler was finalized, deeper conversations have arisen between Kendall and me about her memories of childhood and how she truly feels having a sibling on the severe end of the autism spectrum. She claims that she doesn't spend much time pondering over the subject and she dismisses my attempts at uncovering any resentment or her true feelings. She always reassures me that it doesn't bother her having a sibling with autism. She insists she's never felt disregarded or like she received less attention growing up, which is comforting to hear (even though I know it's not true). I am well aware that the time and focus Skyler requires daily with basic life skills has to be hurtful to Kendall, which is quite understandable. While it's no one's fault, she is always second in line for our attention. Although she frequently acknowledges how much she appreciates the one-on-one time Josh and I make a point to carve out to do things she enjoys, my "mom guilt" simmers incessantly. I don't know how to quell it.

Caring for Ourselves, and Each Other

Without a doubt, one of the best decisions we've made on Kendall's behalf was to encourage her to meet with a therapist. It took roughly two years for her to open up and share honest feedback about what living with autism is truly like from her perspective. She's hyper-focused on being perfect and must succeed at her first attempt of everything she tries or she quits, considering herself a failure. All that self-inflicted pressure has resulted in devastating levels of stress and a clinical diagnosis of anxiety and depression. It's clear to even my medically untrained mind that Kendall is compensating for her brother's disability. She assumes that as long as she keeps straight A's in school, excels at her extracurricular activities, volunteers selflessly at animal shelters (she aspires to be a veterinarian one day), keeps her room tidy and essentially remains a "perfect" child, we won't have additional burdens on our plate worrying about her and Skyler both. I can only imagine how difficult it would be to manage the guilt of being "normal" and the frustration about the many sacrifices you have had to endure because of your special-needs brother. Being a teenager is a time of high emotions for everyone, and Kendall has been doled out an extra helping. I wish I knew how to make this life easier for her.

Now that Kendall is in high school and will be off to college too soon for my liking, she's asked me about the future for her brother. I've assured her that he will continue living with Josh and me until we are no longer physically able to care for him. I hate to think she's already burdening herself with the thought of being his caregiver at the same time she may be married and raising children of her own. To me, that is one of the worst aspects of having a family member with a severe mental or physical disability — ensuring your loved one receives the best care by people who truly love them, which often requires giving up a large piece of your own adult life.

Mentally preparing for Skyler's future is daunting, partly because "aging out" of the therapy centers at the age of 22 is not that far off for him and also because I don't want to self-impose limitations on his potential. Although I fully intend to live forever, reality sets in when we review our wills every few years and ensure that Skyler's Special Needs Trust is in order. The thought of not being around to care for Skyler in his old age can present paralyzing fear. I know I should prepare a detailed plan — which ensures uninterrupted care for Skyler and essentially enables someone to fill our shoes tomorrow, if need be — but I just can't bring myself to do it. In my heart, I believe no one will ever properly attend to him like Josh and I do or mirror the way he's used to us doing things, which I recognize is a problem.

Over the years, I have learned that when you feverishly make plans, God shakes his head ... because only He knows the future and has already cemented His plan for each of us. I just need to be patient (even though I don't have a patient bone in my body!) and trust in God's plan. In the meantime, I know I eventually have to loosen the reins and quiet my inner control freak by letting others *help* us, but that frightens me, too. I'm a doer and I rarely ask for help or relinquish control.

Stepping outside of my faith on occasion, I do sometimes daydream what living with a 25-year-old Skyler would look like. If I could wave a magic wand to create my perfect vision for Skyler's future, it would entail much more independence and a stronger connection with his family, specifically his sister. In an ideal world, Skyler's ability to communicate — even if only through gestures and pointing — would be clear enough that he could ask for what he wants or needs and potentially even have a job where talking isn't a necessity. My heart practically melts every time Kendall offers for Skyler to assist with handling animals in the vet clinic she plans to open after becoming a veterinarian. I think that sounds amazing!

In addition to improving communication, I would love for Skyler to independently handle his daily grooming and personal hygiene (e.g., brushing teeth, getting dressed and showering). I can only imagine the pride he would feel and confidence he would gain by achieving all those tasks without assistance. If all of these dreams for Skyler's growth and development became a reality over the next 10 years, it would lift a significant weight from my shoulders. I believe that it would also dissolve some of the anxiety and fear Kendall holds regarding Skyler's livelihood. I am confident she would attend to his every need and love him dearly in our absence, but I don't want her relationship with Skyler to be only that of his caregiver. However, I would love to see her pick him up for a weekly dinner date or take him grocery shopping. I expect for Kendall to put herself first by fulfilling her many dreams and to not lose sight of her own future plans.

In the meantime, my immediate goal is much smaller and simpler. I dream that my kids can finally take a photo standing next to one another without Skyler being forcefully held or someone getting injured! The things that other families take for granted are my greatest wishes.

CHAPTER SEVEN
The Big Bang Theory

One common assumption is that all people on the autism spectrum are averse to noise, and that loud sounds create sensory overload. But the sensory processing challenges that all children and adults on the spectrum face are themselves a "spectrum." Some kids are the stereo-typical sensory "avoiders" who drive the conventional wisdom about how autism causes kids to retreat from loud noises (or strong scents or bright lights or strong tastes), but other kids are actually sensory "seekers." Skyler seems to crave noise. His incessant open-handed banging on doors, walls, and counters — along with his repeated slamming of drawers and appliances (the microwave door is his personal favorite) — must meet some type of sensory need he has. Perhaps it's the force and pressure to the palms of his hands that he craves, but the accompanying noise gives him so much pleasure that he wears it like a badge of honor in the form of a grin plastered on his face. In addition to producing noise from hitting doors and walls, he takes out his frustration by hitting himself and others, as well as throwing things like couch pillows, dog toys and kitchen utensils.

As a non-verbal young man, Skyler's options for communicating are limited. Without voice or vocabulary, he struggles to tell us what he wants or to gain our attention, so he has many meltdowns and creates mayhem through banging. I, unfortunately, was not blessed with patience, and the loud noises from the constant banging and hitting is annoying and literally drives me to my breaking point. Discipline is not really an option for Skyler because he struggles to make the connection between his action and a negative consequence. Regardless, even if it makes me appear weak or uncaring, I must admit that on many days, I find it difficult to remain calm with Skyler. I sometimes cannot comprehend how a child who needs my assistance with every single daily task could treat me so poorly and not feel any emotion about it. On most days, I think to myself, "Does he even like me?" When he swats my arm as he walks behind me, smacks my leg while we sit next to each other or kicks me when I try to put his diaper on, it literally breaks my heart. I wonder if he'll ever really know who I am or appreciate all that I do for him. I am the person who brought him into this world and who meets his every demand without hesitation. Will he ever utter the word "Mom" or respond to me that he loves me back?

On most days, I think to myself, "Does he even like me?"

It's during some of these moments of hitting and banging that I completely lose my shit, as they say. The reality of autism is stressful and while 90% of the time I handle the daily challenges with a smile and a laugh, I also know I'm human and need to give myself a pass to have an occasional mommy meltdown. I just get to a breaking point where I can't take the abuse and noise anymore and I feel my anger rising like a pressure cooker about to release hot steam. I know that yelling, name calling and smacking his heavily padded behind solves absolutely nothing nor does it reverse negative behavior, but admittedly, I sometimes become overwhelmed by the horrific treatment Skyler frequently dishes out and sometimes, under my breath, I tell him to stop being an asshole. I'm not proud of it, and I feel like the asshole the second after I say it.

I also must be honest about the fact that some days, after enduring hours of being hit and listening to walls, doors and windows being beat on, the minute a therapist arrives at our home to work with Skyler, I sneak away into my bedroom closet, curl up into a ball and ugly cry. In these tearful moments, I'm not exactly sure whether it's the stress from that day, or months of pent-up frustration that triggered me and sent my emotions into overdrive. But it becomes glaringly obvious to me that, although Skyler has made so much progress, he is light years behind kids half his age. I worry so much about the future and whether we'll ever get a break from attending to his every need 24/7. I conclude the cry with a little pep talk to myself.

> *This is my life, and most days it's hard.*
>
> *I'm allowed to make mistakes, express anger and cry.*
>
> *Skyler knows I love him with every fiber of my being.*
>
> *I'm a constant work-in-progress and it's okay to give myself a break,*
>
> *or maybe a time out when I cuss.*

All the hitting and banging has become second-nature to Skyler. It is, after all, his only current form of communication and his primary way to receive attention. I always ask friends and family — who appear shocked when witnessing his behavior — to imagine being extremely frustrated and spending your entire life unable to verbally express why. Skyler is a very smart kid and knows that banging like a wild man brings us eye-to-eye with him to try to comprehend what he is attempting to ask for or determine what is wrong. The majority of the time, without fail, he smirks back at us as if to say, *"Okay, now that you're here, I can stop."*

All the hitting and banging has become second-nature to Skyler. It is, after all, his only current form of communication and his primary way to receive attention.

As a parent of a non-verbal child, I find it beyond frustrating and painful that Skyler is incapable of telling us if he's hungry, tired, has an ache or pain, etc., so we spend day in and day out guessing while his behaviors get louder and more frequent. Over the years, many therapists and physicians have told us that Skyler is just doing it for attention, and that the best course of action is to ignore him, so as to not reinforce the bad behavior. With all due respect to their professional opinions, I highly encourage each and every one of them to spend 24 hours in our home to experience what it's like to live in a household with continuous banging. I guarantee they wouldn't last the full day simply ignoring Skyler's "attention-seeking behavior." Believe me, we have tried not reacting to every single occurrence, except for the times that seemed to correlate with a meal or bedtime, and that "just ignore it" strategy was met with minimal success.

"Mommy, I Don't Feel Good"

An even more painful drawback of Skyler being non-verbal is our inability to know when he's very ill. During the year that I was writing this book, we visited the children's hospital emergency department on multiple occasions because Skyler was visibly suffering, and we had no idea why. There's no, "Mom, I don't feel good" coming from this kid. His tolerance for pain and discomfort is off the charts. The only way we know for sure that he is suffering a bodily injury is noticing a change in his gait or the odd way he may be moving a body part (like a dislocated knee cap when he slipped off a chair in 2014). If Skyler comes down with a flu bug, we aren't usually aware until we wake him in the morning to find that he's covered in vomit. Being that he doesn't understand the concept of making his way, quickly, to the bathroom each time he needs to throw up, Josh and I must gather a stack of towels and prepare to spend hours sitting on either side of him on the couch to help lean him forward and catch the vomit.

One strange and scary incident in 2018 had us freaking out. When I went to wake Skyler for school, I noticed that he had broken out from head to toe in hives. His lips and face were so swollen that I thought his airways would close. Come to find out, he is allergic to sulfa, and the horrible reaction was due to a new medication he was taking that contained sulfa.

A more recent trip to the hospital emergency department had even the physicians puzzled. Skyler couldn't close his mouth to eat or drink anything and was drooling because it was too painful for him to swallow. Our first assumption was strep throat, but his glands were so swollen that the physician worried he may have an abscess in his mouth or throat. To be safe, a CT scan of his neck was ordered, which required sedation. And, despite my advice about how to approach the sedation (practical wisdom learned from several other experiences), the medical professionals proceeded "their way." After the four simultaneous injections of sedation medication were administered into his thighs, he calmed down enough to allow the nurse to swab his throat to run a strep culture test. The results of the CT scan showed no abscess or issues with his throat, and the culture revealed he was positive with a very nasty case of strep throat. If only he could verbalize his aches and pains like a neurotypical child, we could more quickly diagnose and treat his ailments and avoid the multi-hour visits to the hospital (and extra painful, stressful steps like sedation).

If only he could verbalize his aches and pains like a neurotypical child, we could more quickly diagnose and treat his ailments and avoid the multi-hour visits to the hospital (and extra painful, stressful steps like sedation).

In the fall of 2018, when we were first introduced to Skyler's pediatric gastroenterologist, the doctor explained the rationale for much of the banging and hitting was likely due to the GI pain Skyler was experiencing ... which was worsening with age. My first thought was that I, once again, failed Skyler. My child was in horrific pain for the majority of his life, and I didn't demand that other specialists keep looking for causes. My intuition was right — my baby was crying out in pain and fear, and not simply "seeking attention" by being a brat.

Although we've begun treating the symptoms of ulcerative colitis, his most recent diagnosis, the banging has continued as new medications are started and discontinued while we identify the best combination. We are extremely hopeful that his GI specialist can quickly identify a treatment that will change all our lives for the better by reducing the inflammation in his gut and dramatically decreasing the pain he's having.

In the meantime, our goal is to continue teaching Skyler more effective communication methods to identify his wants and needs, but it remains a struggle. When you have been conditioned to hit and bang to have your needs met, and that crosses over into the way you also seek attention, the lines become muddied, forcing us to continue guessing and Skyler's frustration level to reach an all-time high.

Over the years we've tried Big Mac button devices, PECS (picture exchange communication system), iPad apps, sign language, etc. but nothing has been successful. Presenting two choices for food, clothing, activities or toys and having him point to what he wants has made the greatest impact thus far. At the time of this book going to press, we've just made a new PECS book and are trying it again. I might not have all the patience in the world, but I *do* have determination. And I'm never giving up on my son.

> **I might not have all the patience in the world, but I *do* have determination. And I'm never giving up on my son.**

Skyler is very intelligent and knows exactly what he wants and what we are asking of him, but he struggles to effectively communicate. It will definitely take some time and extensive work with his entire team of therapists to teach Skyler a more productive way of requesting things and communicating, but I'm confident he wants to be understood and therefore he'll learn to be more compliant once we find a system that works for us all.

CHAPTER EIGHT

Oh Sh*t!

If you have a weak stomach or simply find the discussion of bowel movements disgusting, I don't blame you. I actually feel the same way. However, when your 17-year-old suffers from Ulcerative Colitis (UC) and is still not potty-trained, poop is a huge aspect of your daily life, and I'd be remiss to eliminate it ... so to speak! Josh and I get through difficult and uncomfortable times by finding the laughter, so I promise you I've generated every possible way to make the topic of poo funny!

For as long as I can remember, Skyler has always suffered from chronic constipation. I was advised to give him a tiny bit of cod liver oil as an infant or toddler, as well as anti-gas drops, to alleviate the bloating and clear signs of bowel backup. If those natural remedies helped, it was only for a day or two, then we were back to the same abdominal distress. Despite his norm of 4-5 days between bowel movements, it always amazes me that from birth, Skyler has mastered the art of bowel explosions at the most inopportune times. His favorite trigger seems to be waiting rooms or lobbies, and he does not discriminate! Like clockwork, the minute we enter the waiting room of any medical office, hair salon or school building, the familiar foul odor hits our noses. Regardless of how equipped our diaper bag is or how much we've mastered the process, panic still sets in. How dirty and gross will the floor be that one of us will surely be kneeling on to handle this mess? Will there be a handicapped stall available for some privacy? More importantly, where did we leave off in our mental "rock, paper, scissors" game to determine who would be tasked with changing him? After all, keeping a tally seemed to be the fairest way to distribute the chore up until Skyler turned 10 or 11, and we no longer felt it appropriate for me to take him into the ladies' room. Prior to that, I would receive countless looks of disgust as to why I would bring a grown boy into the bathroom with me. To try to remain as politically correct as possible (and not add to the growing controversy of gender-neutral bathrooms), Josh unfortunately drew the short straw being the only other male in our family. He became the permanent butt-wiper when we are in public places.

Memorable Catastrophes

Not all our pull-up blow-outs were horrific, but one particular experience a few years ago at a medical appointment sticks with me because I was brought to tears from the overwhelming stress and absurdity of the entire event, which I can certainly laugh at now. First and foremost, we *cannot* do waiting rooms. Skyler refuses to sit down, apparently cannot tolerate magazines fanned out on table tops (they are swiped to the floor in two seconds flat), and he struggles keeping his hands to himself. It also never fails that the doctor is running behind schedule, and the office needs me to fill out forms to update our file. Due to our work schedules, I'm often alone with Skyler for mid-day appointments. Despite repeatedly asking for all intake paperwork to be mailed to me in advance so I can complete it and bring it with me to the appointment, it rarely happens. So, while demonstrating my ninja skills of blocking all of Skyler's attempts to throw things or flee the building, I give the receptionist my usual response, "I'll have to fill the paperwork out later tonight and drop it off tomorrow. We will be out in the hallway walking around until it's our turn, so can you please have the nurse come out and get us?" They reluctantly say it's fine, but honestly, what choice do they have?

On this particular day, during the hallway pacing, I heard Skyler's belly rumbling, and I knew he was preparing to make me earn my butt-wiping badge again. It's impressive really, but like clockwork, his bowel blow-out came the minute we stepped foot into the exam room. I politely asked the nurse to please let the physician know we would be back quickly, and we high-tailed it to the bathroom. I should have known to secure the surroundings of that extremely tight space (place items stored on the back of the toilet or at the sink onto the floor behind me so he couldn't grab them to chuck around the bathroom) before attempting to change Skyler, but I was rushing and I was distracted. I was probably 20 baby wipes in and had broken into a full sweat at this point trying to clean him up and keep the shit from smearing all over me. When I turned to reach for the pull-up in my backpack, he stood up from the toilet seat, turned around and purposely swiped the tray of pre-packaged alcohol swabs directly into the toilet. I tried desperately to keep my cool, but in all honesty, I was seriously losing my figurative shit!

Assuming the doctor had grown tired of waiting and probably skipped us to see the next patient, I hurried to get Skyler dressed and fished the floating alcohol wipes out of the toilet and tossed them into the trash can. We were back in the exam room all of two minutes when I caught a whiff of what I prayed was just a lingering smell from the last poo. Sure as shit — he had another blow-out! Most people probably would've bowed out from the appointment and rescheduled for another day but not this momma! We'd waited months to get onto this doctor's dance card, and I was not about to let some nervous belly explosion send me over the edge (although, at this point, I was teetering). I rushed Skyler back to the bathroom, wiped the sweat from my forehead, and changed him again at a record pace. Upon returning for the third time to the exam room, the doctor had just walked in ahead of us and dismissed the delays as no big deal. It was extremely kind of her to disregard the hard truth that we'd spent twice as much time in the office bathroom as we had the exam room. She conducted her evaluation, adjusted the doses of a few medications and we were on our way. I watched Skyler smile and giggle in my rear-view mirror the entire drive home, seemingly without a care in the world, while I fought back tears of frustration and internally cursed the shitty circumstances (pun intended) we repeatedly deal with.

A more recent sticky situation we found ourselves in involved Skyler's second time aboard an airplane. Ironically, it was our trip to Austin, Texas, for his colonoscopy (an entire poop-themed trip!). The flight to Austin was fantastic because Skyler was required to fast 12 hours before our arrival to town, so there wasn't much in him to eliminate. The colon prep in our hotel room the night before the scope was horrific. If there was ever a time for laughter to keep the mood lighthearted, it was then. Having personally gone through two colon preps, I know how awful it is. But imagine not being potty trained *and* unable to tell anyone you need to get to a bathroom, like pronto. So, for hours, we flanked Skyler as he sat in his stroller (where he's most comfortable chilling) and listened for the thunderous belly rumbling and hilarious fog horn sound of passing gas. Thankfully, we came prepared with what seemed like hundreds of pull-ups and two huge packages of baby wipes because we damn near went through all of it. All of his procedures went well and Skyler was given the "all clear" to travel home the following morning.

I guess it hadn't dawned on us that because Skyler had eaten a few small meals prior to our flight home and was pumped full of

Dulcolax and MiraLAX from the day prior for the colon prep, it was likely he would have a bowel movement during our flight. Midway through the flight, we caught the unpleasant scent we were dreading. Knowing the tiny size of the airplane bathroom, we figured we were up shit creek and would have to suffer through the entire plane ride with a full, foul pull-up. Fearing a coup by the passengers seated around us, I told Josh that it would make the most sense for me to try to change him, seeing as I'm just 5'2 but Josh is 6-feet tall. (In an airplane bathroom, every inch counts! And I think that was the fastest Josh ever agreed with me about anything!). Once Skyler and I got to the back of the plane, I assessed the space and how best to position us. I quickly realized there was no way I could maneuver with the door closed. So, I asked the flight attendant standing nearby if he would be offended if I changed Skyler with the door open. I absolutely hated doing that, but I really had no other option. Without missing a beat, he whispered, "I won't be offended, but you are entitled to your privacy." He told me to wait one second, as he grabbed a blanket from the overhead bin. This amazing man stood in front of the bathroom door — arms extended wide holding the blanket up to block us from other passengers. I was overcome with gratitude and later tweeted about the above-and-beyond experience exhibited by our flight crew — and specifically named that thoughtful flight attendant. Those simple acts of kindness go such a long way and can restore my sometimes-crumbling faith in humanity.

Simple acts of kindness go such a long way and can restore my sometimes-crumbling faith in humanity.

Poopology

Once home from Austin, equipped with some answers and
a treatment plan, we were advised that Skyler's then 16-year battle
with constipation and accompanying intense pain would take quite
some time to reverse. The doctor stressed how crucial it was for us
to perform a monthly colon clean-out just as we had done in preparation for the colonoscopy. I can say with certainty that the process
doesn't get any easier each month for any of us. Josh, Skyler and
I are homebound for basically the entire weekend and are prisoners
confined to the bathroom. If Kendall's not at her dad's, she usually
locks herself in her bedroom, so she doesn't have to smell or observe
the chaos. She says her signal that it's safe to come out of her room
because the ordeal is over is the sound of Skyler's bathtub filling with
water. Although this process is a necessary evil due to his extensive
issues with passing stool, it absolutely breaks our hearts to see him
in such pain. Knowing there's nothing we can do to ease his discomfort aside from clearing out the blockage once a month leaves us
feeling helpless. Also recognizing that Skyler can only communicate
his extreme discomfort by wall banging or exhibiting self-injurious
behaviors (like smacking his thigh super hard hundreds of times)
wears all of us down.

Skyler completed his round of steroid treatment and began taking
a few daily medications — one of which brings more water into his
intestines to make his bowel movements easier to pass. We updated
Skyler's ABA Center about everything and were all beyond excited
to know the abdominal pain is likely the root cause of many of his
negative, aggressive behaviors. After lots of thought and discussion,
Josh and I decided that perhaps the best way to determine whether
Skyler's medications are helping his chronic constipation was to
track the behaviors leading up to a bowel movement and utilize the
Bristol Stool Scale to identify the types of stool he was having at home

and during the day at the ABA Center. Yes, we take detailed notes about the size and consistency of his crap. Because they are amazing humans, his therapists jumped right on board and began adding that information to his daily note for us.

Being a self-professed lover of spreadsheets and because I interpret information more clearly when it's presented visually, I created a graph of all the fecal data gathered over a five-month period to look for trends. (Sure glad I'm putting my MBA degree and analytical skills to good use!) I assumed if we ever wanted to successfully potty train Skyler, we would need to pinpoint the times he was consistently using the bathroom. Frustrating but impactful results came from the graphing, so I am glad I went through all of the trouble. It appeared that regardless of whether Skyler's stool was hard, soft or watery (sorry for the TMI), his self-injury, property destruction and physical aggression ramps up as he is preparing to have a bowel movement. Bottom line, the kid is still suffering greatly, and his conditioned response is to act horribly to diffuse the pain then is all smiles and compliant when the process is over.

Such is life of an autism warrior mom, right? It's safe to say that reducing the agony my child experiences daily from what's supposed to be a natural bodily function has become my new obsession. If it takes daily graphing of stool frequency and performing monthly bowel clean-outs to finally understand the root cause of his aggression and how to alleviate it, consider me knee deep in doodie!

As any loyal *Sesame Street* watcher would understand, this chapter has been brought to you by the letter "P" and the number "2!"

CHAPTER NINE
Family Fun Times

I would be remiss in the writing of
this book to focus only on the *challenges* of raising a child on the autism
spectrum without recognizing the
many amazing moments of laughter
and joy Skyler has brought to our
lives. There are quite a few things
we know he loves but I would doubt
anything ranks above his love for
music and Elmo! I can't even begin
to measure the countless hours of
Sesame Street and "Elmo's World"
DVDs we have watched throughout
the past 17 years and counting.

Skyler watching
"Elmo's World" for probably
the sixth time that day!

While Skyler intensely studies Elmo's every move — with his nose
practically touching the television screen — Josh, Kendall and I are
singing along to the silly songs and top-40 hits recreated with *Sesame
Street*-themed lyrics. To this day, none of us can listen to one of

those popular songs when it comes on the car radio without singing the *Sesame Street* version! I must give kudos to the writers because they've sure found a way to weave in some humor likely understood by only the adults suffering (I mean *appreciating)* the episodes with their kids.

The Soundtrack of Our Lives

Skyler was introduced to many forms of music since he was in utero, but it seemed hip hop always got him kicking and moving around the most. As it turns out, hip hop continues to be his favorite genre even now. During car rides, I throw it back via the Sirius XM 80s and 90s satellite radio stations so Skyler can hear hits from his favorite artists, like Snoop Dogg, 50 Cent, the Black Eyed Peas, Salt-N-Pepa and Sir Mix-a-Lot ... with a little Rick Astley, the Bee Gees, Journey, and Hall & Oats thrown in for good variety. Skyler giggles, rapidly rubs the palms of his hands together and rocks his upper body back and forth, perfectly with the beat ... which makes this former competitive-dancer momma extremely proud that my kid has such great rhythm! Josh, being a true Deadhead, introduced Skyler to the Grateful Dead many years ago, and he really seems to enjoy them. So, during all car rides with Josh, Skyler is exposed to historical Grateful Dead and Dead & Co. concerts via satellite radio.

Recognizing that music was a sure-fire way to make Skyler smile, Josh and I began putting our mad rhyming and freestyling skills to good use by making up impromptu songs about everything from food to baths to using the potty. It's quite impressive, if I do say so myself, that Josh and I can create some pretty amazing lyrics to just about any song on the radio and often develop little jingles from scratch that seem to last through the ages. As much as she has rolled her eyes and begged us to stop "ruining" some of her favorite songs, Kendall has started taking part in the fun by adding in a line or two from time to time.

One of the earliest original creations — which will probably live forever — was Josh's "cheeseburger and mashed potatoes" song originating from Skyler's favorite meal at one of his beloved restaurants: Tucker's in New Albany, Indiana. One Saturday evening after church, we decided to take Skyler out to eat, and we stumbled upon Tucker's. It was practically love at first sight for Skyler. We aren't certain what won him over initially — the over-sized booths, multiple televisions that hung on three large walls, or the incredibly kind staff — but the minute that bun-less cheeseburger and steamy mashed potatoes came out from the kitchen, the kid was overcome with joy! He squealed and cackled after each bite and throughout the entire meal. I'm so proud of us for stepping out of our comfort zone and taking him to a restaurant because what was anticipated as being a highly stressful, potentially overwhelming situation resulted in the discovery of a place that makes Skyler happier than being at Disney World! Now, all we have to say is "Want to go to Tucker's?" and Skyler grins ear to ear. And once we're loaded in the car, the excitement transitions to loud clapping and laughing with each passing mile toward the restaurant exit ramp ... with a little "Baby Got Back" on the radio.

In our family, fun music and great food are our favorite combo. As such, another amazing song (created by yours truly) reflects Skyler's other favorite meal, the naked chicken burrito bowl — which, luckily for us, can be found at the national chain, Qdoba. This kid can devour a burrito bowl like it's his job. We unintentionally introduced the naked burrito concept to him in passing one day when he kept aggressively watching Josh eat his bowl. Skyler pointed at Josh's food repeatedly as if to say "Gimme a bite of that," so he did. At the first taste, Skyler's face lit up like he just discovered a hidden treasure, so we began getting him a bowl of his own anytime we picked up food there. What started as an occasional stop to Qdoba quickly turned into a dinner expectation by Skyler multiple times a week. We collectively named the days that Skyler can expect a Qdoba burrito bowl for dinner as "Taco Tuesdays" and "Fiesta Fridays." Every Tuesday and Friday, the entire ride home from his autism center, "chicken and rice ... no beans, guac, corn, queso and cheese" becomes the chorus to whatever song happens to be playing on the radio. You'd be amazed at how many song melodies can carry those lyrics!

This kid can devour a burrito bowl like it's his job.

Terms of Endearment

At our house, we like silly names as much as we like silly songs. Nearly any situation can warrant the need to make up a silly name, for ourselves, for each other and even for our pets. Likely because he's unable to object, Skyler is no exception to this game and probably has the most nicknames of anyone in our home. Due to our many crazy bathroom situations with Skyler, he's often referred to as "Teddy Fecalman" or, because he is notorious for trying to take off his pants unless they are tied super tight and practically pulled up to his chest, during those situations we have dubbed him "Mr. Pants" or "Captain Britches." Once again, this is a pastime Kendall enjoys participating in and contributing to. Skyler's love of music and his unfortunate hiked-up pants situation had Kendall envisioning Skyler's future career as a club DJ. She bestowed him with the stage names, "DJ Happy Pants" and "DJ Britches," which makes him giggle when she addresses him as such. Skyler's other alter egos include "Clappy," "Fella," "Bubster," "Buddy" and, courtesy of Josh, "Rip Van Tinkle" (when Skyler overflows his pull-up!). Clearly, we don't take ourselves very seriously most of the time and we try to identify the humor in every moment. Most days, we're experts at finding laughter in the daily routine that is our life.

In Search of the Perfect Toy

Skyler has never shown much interest in toys, and the few toys that captured his attention when he was younger were not played with appropriately or as the manufacturer intended. Most often, he would pick up a toy and tap it against his mouth for a few seconds before hurling it like a shot put into the air or against a wall. His favorites were always large musical toys that really left a nice dent when thrown, such as the Fisher-Price See 'n Say, toy guitars, pop-up toys, dolls that spoke (like Tickle Me Elmo) and anything that lit up or played songs when buttons were pushed. His enjoyment of those toys seemed to fade quickly, so I discovered that by rotating out toys he stopped playing with and replacing them with similar toys, it made him forget about the ones out of sight. As soon as the prior favorite toys returned, he was super excited, as if they were brand new.

Completely by accident, I stumbled upon the ultimate toy that — to this day — still brings a huge grin to Skyler's face. While playing with our dog, I grabbed a bumpy ball squeak toy and tossed it for him. Once Skyler heard that squeak noise, he whipped his head around with a huge smile. I kept squeaking the ball, and he laughed uncontrollably. From that point on, the poor dog kept losing the tug-of-war battle over his toys to Skyler. So, when Christmas rolled around that year, without hesitation, I decided to fill both Skyler and the dog's stockings with squeaking dog toys. Whatever it takes to make that beautiful boy of mine belly laugh for hours is worth it, not to mention that many dog toys have lumpy, spiky textures, which are great for sensory stimulation.

Fresh Air and Fresh Perspectives

Despite his love for audio and visual stimulation, Skyler easily gets cabin fever from being cooped up inside for long periods of time.

Often multiple times a day on the weekends, weather permitting, we venture out for some fresh air and exercise with a family walk at one of our many local parks or the pedestrian bridge. Getting Skyler's legs moving

Josh and the "runner guys" representing Team Skyler in the annual Outrunning Autism 5K race

at the start of the walk is the toughest part because he prefers being pushed in his large jogging stroller and is not afraid to demonstrate his irritation with us for making him put in the work. Occasionally, Josh and his amazing friends (who we call "the runner guys") will run and push Skyler in the stroller during some 5K races. Watching Josh cruise along at a ridiculously fast pace while pushing a 125-lb. kid in a 50-lb. stroller is quite a remarkable sight. Skyler also thoroughly enjoys car rides and prefers cruising around shirtless and shoeless. We nicknamed this activity "ridin' dirty." So, whenever we let Skyler know we are heading out to take a drive and inform him that he can ride dirty, he comes running with a huge smile on his face, ready to go. Of course, we sing the chorus of the Ridin' (Dirty) song by Chamillionaire when buckling him in the car.

I wish I could properly describe the bond Skyler and Josh share. I truly believe they were destined to be in each other's lives. Besides constantly singing to Skyler, Josh wrestles with him and moves Skyler's arms around while providing commentary like a ventriloquist. A family favorite is when Josh speaks in his best Italian accent pretending that Skyler is the Pope. Josh has Skyler saying phrases like "Imma the Pope-ah, bless you in da name of the Fadder, da Son and da Holy Ghost" while moving Skyler's arms through the sign of the cross — trust me, it's quite hilarious to witness. Every one of these activities makes Skyler laugh so hard he snorts and squeals. Of course, when Josh is out of town for work, and I'm trying to get Skyler to laugh, I reenact some of Josh's wrestling moves, which is met with barely a smile but otherwise total silence. It always reminds me of the scene from the movie *Liar Liar* when Jim Carrey does "The Claw" with his son, and when the mother's boyfriend tries to imitate the

Josh and Skyler
walking in the park
....

move, the child looks at him like he's so dumb. Same thing. Skyler looks at me as if to say, "Nice try, Mom, but you are not Josh."

All the stress and frustration that Autism causes families can be overwhelming and downright irritating. Our family focus is to make every situation as light-hearted as possible and to find the FUNNY! As Josh and I always say to one another, "If we don't laugh, we'll probably cry," so we choose laughter every time.

CHAPTER TEN

This Is Why We Can't Have Nice Things

Often times, I look around my house and my eyes focus in on where the walls are covered in scuff marks or dents. I can't help but scrutinize the floors that have tiny chips of wood missing or realize that, unlike most homes where the youngest children are teenagers, we still have child gates in most doorways. Each of the bruises on our home has a story to tell and it is highly probable that the majority of stories trace back to Skyler's autism-related behaviors.

To gain attention, Skyler enjoys throwing things. Most days I feel like I'm speaking to a toddler and repeating the phrase "No sir, don't throw that," which he ignores. When he was little and couldn't reach counters and table tops, he would throw toys. The toys that piqued Skyler's interest at the time were the large, heavy, musical toys that could really do some damage when chucked across the room into a wall. The organizer in me rationalized that maybe keeping his toys contained (versus scattered around his room) would lessen his desire to pick them up and toss them, so I bought one of the multi-colored bin organizers and prayed for "out of sight, out of mind." But like most of my bright ideas, it was fated for failure. Skyler found it even more entertaining to pull each plastic bin full of toys off the stand and hurl it across the room. "Point, set, match!"

Deck the Halls

As much as I love Christmas time, the thought of tree decorating used to give me great anxiety. I thoroughly enjoy trimming the tree, but I lost countless ornaments over the years because Skyler couldn't help but pluck one off the tree each time he walked past. And what was plucked was quickly broken. It's like those pretty ornaments were calling his name, and he had to touch them. Again, attempting to outsmart him, I decided to take all the high-back bar stools and arrange them in a circular formation around the bottom of the tree, which blocked his little hands from actually reaching the branches. Mind you, this looked absolutely ridiculous, but I had tunnel focus and was committed to winning. This worked for a few days until he figured out how to wiggle his tiny arm in the small space between the rungs of the chairs to get at the ornaments again. Needless to say, the tree came down the day after Christmas that year.

The following year, I conceded defeat and opted to only decorate the top 1/3 of the Christmas tree, which — again — looked completely ridiculous. However, it achieved multiple goals. Our family was able to enjoy a semi-decorated tree, and the décor was out of his line of sight and mostly out of reach. It was important to me that I not let Skyler's busy hands ruin for Kendall the experience of decorating our family Christmas tree together. Skyler proved resilient and would stand on his tip toes, hang onto a branch and practically pull the tree over while trying to reach an ornament at the top. After eight or nine years of failed ideas, I was fed up. For every Christmas that followed, you would find an ornament-free, pre-lit tree in our main living room and a second smaller tree fully decorated in the basement living area, where Skyler doesn't often go. Mom win! #GoodEnough

A Cyclone of Activity

A huge irritation for Skyler is not having our full attention 24/7. He is extremely impatient (what kid isn't, really?) and very calculated, which sometimes makes for a wicked combination when you're a kid who is unable to verbalize what you want or need. I try extremely hard to complete all the work required by my full-time job prior to picking Skyler up from his autism center; however, on rare occasions, I may have a quick conference call or email to handle as soon as we get home. I'll let Skyler select a *Sesame Street* DVD to watch, and as soon as the video begins, he scans the room to make sure I'm located nearby to watch it with him. Once he's engaged deeply into his movie, I quickly depart to accomplish my quick task, but the minute I leave the room, the acting out begins. If I'm in my home office, Skyler will go into the kitchen, which is his favorite place to practice his shot-put skills, pull spatulas from the utensil holder on the counter and send them sailing, one by one, across the room. If that doesn't elicit a response from me, he will slam cabinet doors, drawers, the microwave or refrigerator door over and over again or throw any dishes and silverware that happen to be in the sink to the floor. If instead of the office, I dash into our master bedroom for a quick second to change my clothes, Skyler will go into the office, grab a handful of pens or loose papers from my desk and scatter them to the floor. Another favorite pastime of Skyler's is to throw all the pillows from the couch around the room. In his defense on that one, they *are* called "throw pillows." He'll continue with this behavior until

I come face-to-face with him, giving him the one-on-one attention he desires.

Skyler clearly finds great joy in throwing things and acting out for attention because, after all, it is a learned behavior that has always successfully achieved the result he desires. We continually try to eliminate the objects and opportunities to curtail this negative behavior, but Skyler is resilient and finds new items he feels need relocating to the floor. It's not only exhausting monitoring his every move, but worrisome. We have recently begun working with another behavioral therapist who sees Skyler both at the ABA Center and in our home. She has already demonstrated for us some impactful ways to redirect his propensity for throwing and hitting. I have a strong suspicion the next round of points will be awarded to Mom!

It's not only exhausting monitoring his every move, but worrisome.

Do Not Pass Go

The damage to the walls and floors is easy to overlook, but the barricades throughout our house are both an eyesore and a traffic nightmare. Within the past few years, we have resorted to purchasing several baby gates to block off certain rooms in the house because of the cyclone of damage Skyler can cause. Prior to the gates, if the bathroom door was mistakenly left open, Skyler would pull down towels from the towel bar; unravel toilet paper and eat it; and throw toothbrushes, hand soap, tissues and shampoo all within about a 5-second timespan. If Skyler is accidentally permitted into the forbidden land of Kendall's room, all hell breaks loose should he touch or rearrange (to the floor) any of her things. Our solution was to place the gates across the lower portion of a doorway or top of a stairwell. Oddly enough, Skyler views these gates as impassable and is deterred from trying to gain entry; he never steps over them or climbs them. Although the gates serve their purpose in containing Skyler and protecting our house and our possessions, the gates are extremely annoying for the rest of us to constantly bypass, especially Kendall and me because we are vertically challenged and can't hike our legs up to clear them like six-foot Josh can. It's beyond frustrating living in a home seemingly filled with booby traps when trying to quickly go room to room, but Skyler's inability to control his hands dictates this solution as necessary. I'm a runner, not a hurdler, but I'm learning ...

CHAPTER ELEVEN

Socializing – The Struggle is Real

I read a funny social media meme the other day that said: "All these other moms are talking about honor roll, dance recitals, softball games, gymnastics meets and I'm sitting here like: Woo Hoo! She tried a new food *and* her socks didn't bother her!"

Perhaps we can relate in one way or another about personal victories seeming small or insignificant when compared to others. I truly believe social media is a tremendous platform for personal connection and even business development and issues advocacy, but the downside (besides trolls and bullies) is assuming that the glorious vacations, countless cocktail parties, daily fitness achievements, and flawless family and self-portraits represent the honest and perfect daily life of friends and acquaintances.

I can fully admit feeling envious and sometimes saddened when I see the posts of friends' teenagers hitting up the DMV to get their driver's licenses or the mega-watt smiles of kids posing for group shots for homecoming or prom. Skyler was born at the same time as all of them and, as toddlers, they used to have play dates together. At that time, actually play dates were more for my mom friends and me to get the heck outta the house and drink some wine! So it's extremely difficult for me to watch all these young men and women move on to experience the fun rites of passage most parents look forward to ... while Josh and I sit on the sidelines, just hoping our son will one day say his first word or feed himself independently. A friend and fellow special-needs momma perfectly captured my feelings when she said to me, "Being a special-needs parent is just constantly grieving over what might have been. It's just hard."

> **"Being a special-needs parent is just constantly grieving over what might have been. It's just hard."**

Small Talk and Big Challenges

It's often awkward when I meet someone for the first time and, while exchanging introductions and pleasantries, they ask, "Do you have children?" I generally reply the same way with, "I sure do. I have a daughter who is 15 and a son who is 17." Inevitably, they respond back with, "Oh, I bet you are extremely busy with sports and all the craziness of high school, but I bet your son helps out with some of the chauffeuring, right?" It's at that point that I take a deep breath and have to decide what type of explanation I'm feeling up to sharing that day.

I'll be completely honest — most of the time, it's just easier to say something like, "Yep, teenagers make our lives kind of crazy" or "We are definitely always on the go" ... because both of those statements are actually true. We *are* always on the move, and both kids frequently drive us bat-shit crazy! I then dwell on my response for the remainder of the day and night, wondering if I'm doing Skyler a disservice for not just coming out with it. "My son is actually autistic and doesn't attend a traditional school, doesn't play any sports, and will most likely never learn to drive. In fact, he's never uttered a single word in his entire life and he's not potty trained."

Too heavy? Too real? Yeah, exactly what I think, and the reason why I give a standard answer similar to "I'm fine" when someone asks how I'm doing. The crazy part of the "I'm fine" type of response is that, in my mind, it's most often given out of habit or reflex because people are frequently asking only to make polite conversation and don't actually want to hear — in detail — how a person is doing. It's not that they don't care. But, well, yeah ... maybe they don't care. It's too much.

I can concede that my way of thinking likely makes me sound like Debbie Downer, but I honestly believe people would regret asking me anything about my life in the future, if I told the God's-honest truth instead of a canned response. I also don't want the pity expression that follows when I describe that my 17-year-old has severe autism and all that goes along with that. So, I have learned to allow the green-eyed monster to sneak into my thoughts for a split second when viewing all the special moments posted by friends on Facebook. To have a tinge of jealousy is normal and surely doesn't take anything away from the true joy and genuine happiness I feel for all of Skyler's former playmates moving on with their lives. I'm only human, and I know there is nothing wrong with mourning those rites of passage that I'll never get to experience with my son. What I get to experience instead is unconditional love from a child who needs me to assist with every single aspect of his day.

I'm only human, and I know there is nothing wrong with mourning those rites of passage that I'll never get to experience with my son.

Maybe the inability to talk about my real life in full detail when making small talk with strangers and casual acquaintances was a motivator for me to write this book. Our story is important and I know that other people will find it full of epiphanies or support or at least a window into how other people live. But it's not a story I know how to tell in a few minutes, in passing at the mall or the library. I hope all the people I've had to tell "just enough" will read this book to find out more. And I hope they'll call or connect and help me find my way back, if I'm having a hard day, to seeing the silver linings, like how nice it is to know that Skyler will never steal my car and stay out all night partying with his friends.

Parties, Outings and Vacations

Skyler's lack of social awareness presents quite a challenge for Josh and me when trying to venture out into our community with him for dinners, errands or even literal walks in the park. Never knowing what triggers may send Skyler into a meltdown keeps us from accepting many invitations we receive for parties, cookouts and oodles of other events that include our entire family. It's no fault of theirs, but we sometimes feel isolated from friends and family. The conundrum for us is this: Do we continue turning down invitations and run the risk of no longer being included (because we always decline) or do we take them at their word when they say "Bring Skyler ... he can't hurt anything" and stress out through the entire experience, watching him like a hawk and terrified that, despite our best efforts, he'll leave a trail of damage? Due to significant lack of respite care providers or babysitters, our usual plan of action is to take turns attending events solo and only on the rarest of occasions attend functions as a family.

We sometimes feel isolated from friends and family.

Bringing Skyler to a private party or public event is not as easy as people assume. The situation requires that Josh and I divide and conquer. One of us will stay close to Skyler, following him around every minute, ensuring he doesn't break things, pull hair or hit. Meanwhile, the other parent tries to socialize. It's honestly miserable for all of us because we are so on edge that no one can relax and enjoy themselves. Most days, it's just easier to stay home. We were homebodies long before the global pandemic made it a necessity.

Josh and I have a lot of energy and a lot of Skyler-management skills, but the hardest part is sometimes emotional. You see, venturing out in public also opens our family up to critical glances and unfair judgment from people who assume they know our situation just by watching. It honestly makes me crazy when people tell me they had no idea Skyler had autism because he doesn't "look disabled." What would be nice is if those same individuals staring me down and watching me struggle to get his stroller through a door or keep him from running off while I'm trying to sign him in for a medical visit would, instead, come over and ask me if I could use a hand. The answer is "Yes!" I can promise you that many parents with special-needs children would be extremely appreciative and jump at the chance for a little assistance. Even if they were to say "No, thank you ... I've got this," the simple attempt of kindness would make their day. Collectively, such kindness and grace can make the world a better place. Okay, getting off my soap box now.

Clearly, Josh and I can't turn down every invitation we receive and we can't avoid leaving the house entirely. So we *plan*. Determined to make family outings a more frequent occurrence, Josh and I spend considerable time and effort preparing for every possible scenario. We always say, "What's the worst thing that could happen?" Then we plan for that times two! One night after church, with our frustrations divinely lifted and fleeting patience from a long day restored, we decided to throw caution and worry to the wind and test out our pre-planned scenario by going out to dinner. This was the night we discovered Tucker's, Skyler's now-favorite restaurant. Being that it's a sports-themed restaurant equipped with multiple televisions on every wall, we knew the high level of noise already resonating throughout the room would allow Skyler to blend in nicely if he started banging on the table. He did fairly well by eating most of his bun-less cheeseburger and kept his table banging and incessant clapping to a moderate level. I believe he was so in awe of eating dinner any place other than the kitchen table that he was too distracted to act the fool.

> **Clearly, Josh and I can't turn down every invitation we receive and we can't avoid leaving the house entirely. So we *plan*.**

We should have quit while we were ahead. Feeling far too cocky and confident about our son's excellent behavior, we decided to try another restaurant outing the following weekend, which proved to be a complete shit show. Everything that could've gone wrong did. The minute we sat down, Skyler threw the condiments to the floor, loudly banged his hands repeatedly on the table — causing most of the patrons to stare at my bratty kid who they likely felt needed better discipline (insert eye roll). Then Skyler proceeded to spit out the food he normally loves for God-only-knows what reason, and kept grabbing food from our plates, which he threw instead of ate.

We were beyond pissed, frustrated, embarrassed — basically feeling *all* the emotions. Later that evening when our irritation and anger had passed, Josh broke any lingering tension by inserting humor per usual with, "I guess he prefers Tucker's?"

Over a good chuckle while recapping the craziness, Josh and I vowed to not give up or dwell on this one rough incident but, instead, focus on the valuable lessons learned during that second experience. Here's what we learned, and the new rules we instituted:

1. If the restaurant has a wait, we need to burn off some energy. Now, Josh walks Skyler around the parking lot or sits with him listening to music in the car until receiving a text from me that we are being seated.

2. First order of business after being seated at the booth (must always be a booth!) is to remove all condiments, utensils and menus from Skyler's reach.

3. Always order Skyler's food when the drink order is taken because his waiting game is *not* strong.

4. The parent who is assisting Skyler with eating should always order their meal with a to-go container because the Prince of Impatience will definitely *not* allow said parent to eat. When Skyler's finished, we need to go!

5. Request the bill the minute the food is presented at the table.

6. While one parent pays the bill, the other parent walks Skyler very carefully, hands pressed to his sides, out of the restaurant ... ensuring he doesn't swipe drinks or food from other tables to the floor.

Following those essential steps (and ensuring Tucker's is always in the restaurant rotation) is the only way we can enjoy dinner out of our home. While it may seem overwhelming to read, it has become our normal routine, which is second nature to us now.

But if a night out is a production, a day or three must be impossible, right? Yeah, sort of. On the extremely rare occasion that schedules align and we agree on a destination, Josh and I jump at any chance we have to get away for a much-needed vacation. The only people we feel comfortable leaving Skyler with for several days and nights are my sister, Beth, and my 22-year-old niece, Maddie, who both live in Michigan. A few years ago, we asked Maddie if she would be comfortable watching Skyler for a week (Josh had won another fabulous trip to Ireland!), and she quickly agreed. She would be the first person to ever stay with Skyler for that length of time, so you better believe I left her a 5-page list of notes and instructions. There are so many little things about his routine that we just know to do, but the extent of his daily care is foreign to anyone who does not live it or spend extensive time observing us.

For Maddie, it was a quick learning curve — early-morning wake-up calls, lots of laundry, all the bed wetting, the dinners, the baths and the bedtime routine. She went from taking care of only herself to being an instant mom for what surely felt like a very *loooooong* week. Skyler seemed to enjoy her company and behaved well, as least that's what she told us, but admittedly she was exhausted by the time we returned. Skyler was at his ABA center full-time during the days, so she had some time for napping and catching up, but it's never quite enough ... we know!

It was somewhat comforting to hear Maddie's perspective on just how difficult it was to understand what Skyler wants, thinking you've figured it out only to be repeatedly wrong with your assumptions ... which then makes him upset. We were eternally grateful for our brief break from reality and weren't surprised to hear she slept for a solid 16 hours after returning home! If nothing else, she did gain some valuable hands-on experience for her college degree — a BS in Speech, Language and Hearing Sciences. I wish she could have received course credit!

Last year, my sister, who somehow inherited much more patience than I did, offered to come down and spend the week with Skyler and Kendall so Josh and I could get away. She has always been the first person I've called when needing parenting advice or ideas, and I knew both kids would enjoy all the fun activities she would come up with. Being that she's a mother and has been a middle school teacher for 25 years, I didn't think she needed the extensive five pages of notes I left for her daughter; however, I did suggest that she come down a day early to watch us do some of the daily routine things. All went well as expected, but she, too, left exhausted.

When we spoke a few days later, she told me that she was continually thinking about her time with Skyler and repeatedly mentioned that she doesn't know how we handle all the day-to-day requirements of Skyler along with Kendall's school and dance schedule, our full-time jobs, etc. without losing control and becoming overwhelmed. She went on to say that it was such an eye-opening experience to walk in our shoes, which was quite different from assuming she understood our life just by observing or hearing us talk about it in conversation. Finally, she told me how proud she was of me as a mother and that my children are extremely lucky to have Josh and me as parents. That very heartwarming sentiment coming from the big sister I have always looked up to meant the world to me and confirmed that, although parenting a special-needs child can be difficult, our hard work and patience hasn't gone unnoticed.

CHAPTER TWELVE

Devotion to Self and a Healthy Marriage

Maintaining a household with two children under the age of five was challenging, particularly when the bulk of each day revolved around the demanding schedule and minute-to-minute care required by a special-needs child. I quickly became physically and emotionally exhausted. Add to that being a single parent for several years between my separation from the kids' biological father and my marriage to Josh, and I was burning the candle at both ends, barely functioning inside or outside of our home and had absolutely no energy left to devote to self-care. Instinctually, we as parents put the needs of our children first, but it's just not sustainable over the long term.

> **Instinctually, we as parents put the needs of our children first, but it's just not sustainable over the long term.**

For me, running is salvation from the stress. It was my love before I became a mother and it was important that I maintain my identity as a runner after I became a mother too. I initially started running short distances while in college but decided to conquer my first full marathon the spring of 2002, the year before Skyler was born. Although the race course was extremely hilly, and it poured rain for the last 14 of the 26.2 total miles, it was exhilarating. When I received that medal around my neck at the finish line, I had that runner's high most long-distance runners speak of ... and I was hooked. Finding out I was pregnant with Skyler soon after completing that race was so exciting. He entered my world almost a year to the date of that marathon. As you already know by now, the two years leading up to Kendall's birth were consumed with therapy and medical appointments and navigating our entrance into the world of autism.

Reclaiming My "Me Time"

I distinctly remember what my life looked and felt like right after Kendall was born. Managing a newborn and two-year-old with significant developmental delays was exhausting and taking quite a toll on my physical and mental health. I would go many days without eating and I was drowning in a sea of uncertainty and worry. Deep down, I knew that getting my sanity under control with some physical activity was vitally important to not only lengthen my life span, but as an essential requirement for managing stress. Knowing all that was well and good, but how in the hell could I justify to my judgmental self that it was okay (and damn-near *critical*) that I carve out some brief "me time" each day? With a full-time job outside of the home and a husband who was minimally helpful with housework and parenting (remember, I was still married to my first husband at this point), where would I find even an extra five minutes to take care of myself?

It seemed impossible to fit one more thing into my schedule, but I knew that self-care mattered now more than ever. Luckily, I had some mental and physical "muscle memory" in this regard. Throughout my youth, whether it be conditioning for my competitive dance team or taking a break while cramming for college exams, running and exercising always provided clearness of mind, improved my patience and calmed my anxiety. Something about the solitude of just me and the undetermined path or mileage I'd complete — accompanied by only the up-tempo music pumping through my earphones — provided such clarity and perspective to the situations causing me anguish. Repeatedly envisioning that scenario that I enjoy so much finally gave me the kick in the pants I needed to get my running shoes back out and grant myself permission to put myself first. I confidently told Skyler and Kendall's dad about my intentions and I coordinated my running schedule to be the least disruptive to the family as possible (running early on weekends before they all woke up, doing evening runs on the treadmill when the kids were asleep, etc.). Clearly, by being so accommodating, I was still demonstrating guilt for making myself a priority, but I considered it a baby step toward gaining a piece of myself back and a win/win for everyone.

I'm naturally a very competitive person, so when I decide to tackle any challenge, I make it a big one. Getting back into running after a two-year hiatus had me sitting in a front-row seat on the struggle bus, which was to be expected. If you don't use it, you lose it and going from zero running to trying to run a mile without gasping for air was a shock to my slightly malnourished and deconditioned frame. After a few three-mile jogs (which weren't so bad), I felt that runner's high creeping back into me. In no time flat, I had the itch to do another marathon. For ol' competitive me, it wouldn't be good enough to just *complete* another marathon; I intended to come back stronger and faster than before, beating my prior finishing time, so I certainly had my work cut out for me.

The Chicago Marathon

Identifying my next marathon destination was easy. I needed a fast and flat course with lots of crowd support, and I was looking for a location that wasn't terribly far away from home. The 2007 Chicago Marathon perfectly fit all my criteria and allowed me six solid months of training until race day. While preparing my training schedule, I was a little anxious about the intense amount of mileage I would need to work back up to after two pregnancies and virtually no wear-and-tear on my running shoes for the past four years. However, I kept reminding myself that it was honestly the only time throughout my day when I could get away from thinking about therapists, seizures and autism, so putting on those headphones and hitting the pavement was a fantastic release and a personal challenge that I was once again ready to tackle. I *needed* to tackle it.

The many weeks of double-digit mileage passed quickly and I met some great new running friends along the way who were supportive and encouraging. I remember being so excited for this race in particular because I had joined forces with an autism organization and

Laurie at the 2007 Chicago Marathon, with Skyler's photo on her racing singlet raised thousands of dollars for the cause. As race day drew closer, I thought through every detail down to pre-planning my racing clothes. I was thrilled to find a local printing business willing to screen-print a photo of Skyler onto my racing singlet. Even though he couldn't be there, he would run the race alongside me, encouraging me with each step just as I had encouraged him months earlier as he learned to walk.

Despite all my training, planning and preparation, I was bested by the one unpredictable factor for any event — the weather. This particular year, it was unseasonably hot for October. Temperatures soared into the upper 80s (which is prohibitively hot for distance running) and hundreds of runners fell ill during the race. One 35-year-old man died. For the first time in its 30-year history, the Chicago Marathon was halted before everyone had reached the finish line. The suspension of the race set off waves of confusion and chaos. For those of us who were beyond the halfway point, officials allowed us to proceed running or walking to the finish line at our own discretion. While I had no chance of beating my prior marathon time, I refused to quit and be loaded up on one of the many air-conditioned buses parked along the course for our convenience. Even if I walked the last few miles, I had to complete what I started. I felt well enough to make it, so I kept going. The minute I crossed the finish line in Chicago, I burst into tears. I was both proud of my accomplishment and also overcome with emotion — and likely heat exhaustion — wishing Skyler would've been there, so I could embrace him to share the joy of it all.

Running Toward a New Future

In the months that followed that huge personal victory, I identified that I was still struggling with depression and anxiety. I was overwhelmed about the future of my personal life (knowing my marriage to my first husband was coming to an end) and I was coming to terms with our autism truth: that the prognosis for Skyler's future development wasn't improving. Before making any drastic, life-altering decisions, I sought the assistance of a psychologist and quickly learned a very important phrase; "You must be selfish before you can be selfless," she told me. After several months of soul searching and self-reflection, in late 2008, I decided to file for divorce.

Reflecting back on that time, it seems obvious to me now that crossing that Chicago Marathon finish line was symbolic and actually the confidence boost that I needed. I knew it was time to escape the unhappy, lonely life I was living and demonstrate for my kids a more joyful, considerate and loving home, even if it meant doing it as a single mom. I finally believed I was strong enough.

The year following the divorce was a watershed moment of personal and professional self-discovery. I evaluated every aspect of my life, including my friendships and my career path, removing as much toxicity as possible. I implemented a new "normal" for our family of three — me, Skyler and Kendall — by remaining focused on raising two amazing and happy little people while continuing to rebuild my self-worth. Being a very detail-oriented person who enjoys making a daily schedule and checking each item off as it's completed (i.e., having a naturally controlling personality), I know I'm more likely to go for a run or carve out "me time" if it's on the schedule. Say what you will about not living spontaneously, but one of those scheduled running days ultimately led me to meet my marathon-loving, soon-to-be second husband, Josh.

Many of our first conversations revolved around running and our careers, which are in the same industry. It was so refreshing to talk to someone with whom I shared so many similar interests, and someone who could relate to my work experiences as well. In 2011, after about a month of dating, I mentioned to Josh that I had signed up to run two marathons that were six weeks apart — Columbus,

OH, and Indianapolis, IN. He thought I was slightly crazy, but being a supportive boyfriend, he pumped me up for both races and even ran the second half of the Indianapolis marathon right by my side, shouting encouragement at every mile marker leading up to the finish. With each race, my completion time kept improving, becoming a "personal record" (PR), which was exciting. You see, I had my sights set on qualifying for the Boston Marathon in the not-so-distant future.

Over the past 18 years, I've run 10 full marathons, countless half marathons and smaller local races, was a fitness instructor, became a CrossFit enthusiast and competed in a body-building competition at the age of 43. Through it all, I've gained as much mental strength as I have gained physical strength. For the first time in my life, I feel confident and secure in who I am as a person and the decisions I make as a mother.

It seems I will always be searching for the newest workout craze or will occasionally head out for a quiet run, but regardless of what Josh and I do for exercise, we know it must be something. Breaking a sweat together in our garage gym or separately is one of our means of self-care and definitely releases a lot of the tension and stress we feel trying to care for everyone else. In fact, most Sunday evenings, Josh and I compare work and family calendars in true "Laurie fashion" in order to schedule the best times for each of us to work out — which is a far cry from my days of feeling selfish for even *wanting* to step away from all things autism for some alone time.

Prioritizing Marriage and Family

Allowing ourselves an outlet for exercise and self-care is important, but an equal priority to us from the day we said "I do" is nurturing our marriage during challenging circumstances and not neglecting our relationship. It takes excessive amounts of energy to care for our children, ourselves and a healthy marriage when our patience is routinely tested. We've learned the hard way that even when it may be difficult, open and honest communication and support for one another is a must. By default, our intention is to model for Skyler and Kendall what a unified, strong relationship looks like, hopefully providing them with a sense of security about the future.

> **Our intention is to model for Skyler and Kendall what a unified, strong relationship looks like, hopefully providing them with a sense of security about the future.**

Having already endured one failed marriage, I now recognize how gravely important it is to have your efforts appreciated by your spouse, which goes both ways. Although one of my "Love Languages" (with a nod to the brilliant Gary Chapman for his book) is "acts of service" — and I should therefore be overjoyed to have extra help — I had become so accustomed to doing *everything* for my son that it was still hard for me to "allow" Josh's acts of service to include taking care of Skyler. I have had to redefine my role as Skyler's "exclusive" caregiver and sometimes step aside when Josh wants to provide assistance or take over some of the daily tasks required by Skyler. Rather than resist the help and later complain that I'm feeling depleted or resentful, sharing the responsibilities and giving credit for Josh's effort has definitely made us feel more like a team.

We have made countless attempts to set up a standing "date night" at least one Saturday night each month. It has not been easy to follow through on that plan, due to lack of caregivers offering respite assistance (short-term relief for anyone providing primary support to a family member in need) for Skyler, but now that Kendall is old enough, she occasionally offers us some time away. Her main stipulations for "watching" Skyler are that we cannot leave until he is asleep (he prefers to go to bed at 7:30 p.m., so that's not often an issue), and we cannot be gone more than two or three hours in case he wakes up.

As great as date nights can be, there are many circumstances that make them an impossible option. Trying to be more practical, we like to carve out creative ways to spend quality time together in the comfort of our own home. Sometimes we will both take a vacation day from work and lounge around the pool while the kids are in school. I mean, who wouldn't appreciate a few hours to catch up on all the long-lost sleep in a quiet home? Occasionally, we'll really get crazy on a Saturday night and after Skyler goes to bed (and actually is sleeping), I'll pour a glass of wine and snuggle up with Josh on the couch to Netflix and Chill ... as the kids say.

Maintaining a close and healthy relationship with Kendall is also vital to the stability and mental health of our family. We have never wanted her to feel isolated or to feel as if Skyler was more important because he requires so much of our time and assistance. In order to combat any potential feelings of resentment she could develop toward her brother or me, I instituted "Mommy and Kendall" time back when the kids were very young. Two Saturday nights a month, she would camp out in my bed, and we watched Disney movies and ate popcorn. She always got so excited on Friday nights and would excitedly confirm, "Tomorrow is our sleepover, right?"

As Kendall got older, we would spend a Saturday getting our nails done, going out to eat or attending a movie she was eager to see. Early into our relationship, Josh was always great about pushing us out the door and voluntarily spending the day with Skyler so the girls could have their alone time.

Once we were married, Josh and I began trading off spending one-on-one time doing fun activities with Kendall. Looking back, I'm elated that he quickly became so involved in the lives of both Skyler and Kendall because the bond shared between the kids and Josh resembles exactly what a father/child relationship should be.

I recognize how blessed I am to have found a loving partner willing to take on the challenges that come with raising a special-needs son as well as a busy, hilarious and sarcastic neurotypical daughter. No marriage is perfect or likely easy, but I've definitely found the person I want running alongside me for the rest of my life.

My Life in Pictures

2009 San Antonio Marathon

2010 Detroit Marathon

2012 Rock 'n' Roll New
Orleans Marathon

"Give 5 Minutes for Autism"
Nationwide CrossFit Event

2015 Outrunning Autism 5K with the "Runner Guys"

2016 — Josh's fourth time
running the Boston Marathon

CHAPTER THIRTEEN

A Purposeful Life

For those not living in what feels like an autism bubble, I hope you now have a much better idea of what challenges and blessings we face raising loved ones on the spectrum. As it's often said, "If you've met one person with autism, you've met one person with autism" — meaning this is not a cookie-cutter diagnosis with a one-size-fits-all treatment approach. Each person diagnosed with Autism Spectrum Disorder is unique and should be treated as such. If you are a parent or family member living and learning from this puzzling disorder, I hope that my autism journey grants you some peace in knowing that although it can be a long and frustrating road, you are not traveling it alone. I hope that the stories in this book have made you feel genuinely welcomed into my life.

Keep seeking out more stories, more insights and more connections. There is so much support available today that, even 17 years ago when Skyler was born, simply didn't exist. The autism community is full of so many stories like mine — some families just recently receiving their diagnosis and some with more than 30 years of experiences. The fabulous part of connecting and sharing is how much we can learn from one another! I cannot promise things will get easier or that any therapies and treatments that proved unsuccessful with Skyler over the years won't work for your child or loved one. Try what makes sense. Be hopeful and realistic. What I do know for certain is that you will likely become overwhelmed, especially if you can't identify and accept the humor in some situations. A bit of laughter can calm even the most stressful of times and helps keep the parental relationship from deteriorating when frustrations are misdirected at each other.

Loving and caring for Skyler is the hardest job I've ever done, but I wouldn't trade my life for anyone else's. I could easily dwell on the hardships we face, but that only brings a negative energy around all of us and defeats my purpose of living a fulfilling life with a grateful heart.

Loving and caring for Skyler is the hardest job I've ever done.

I am often asked to describe the experience of raising a special-needs child and until writing this book, I didn't have something I could hand to people and say "It's like this ... welcome to my life." So I used to suggest people read this 1987 poem entitled "Welcome to Holland" by Emily Perl Kingsley. It sums up perfectly what special-needs parenting is all about.

Welcome to Holland[1]

By Emily Perl Kingsley

I am often asked to describe the experience of raising a child with a disability — to try to help people who have not shared that unique experience to understand it, to imagine how it would feel. It's like this ...

When you're going to have a baby, it's like planning a fabulous vacation trip — to Italy. You buy a bunch of guide books and make your wonderful plans. The Coliseum. The Michelangelo David. The gondolas in Venice. You may learn some handy phrases in Italian. It's all very exciting.

After months of eager anticipation, the day finally arrives. You pack your bags and off you go. Several hours later, the plane lands. The flight attendant comes in and says, "Welcome to Holland."

"Holland?!?" you say. "What do you mean Holland?? I signed up for Italy! I'm supposed to be in Italy. All my life I've dreamed of going to Italy."

But there's been a change in the flight plan. They've landed in Holland and there you must stay.

The important thing is that they haven't taken you to a horrible, disgusting, filthy place, full of pestilence, famine and disease. It's just a different place.

So you must go out and buy new guide books. And you must learn a whole new language. And you will meet a whole new group of people you would never have met.

It's just a different place. It's slower-paced than Italy, less flashy than Italy. But after you've been there for a while and you catch your breath, you look around … and you begin to notice that Holland has windmills … and Holland has tulips. Holland even has Rembrandts.

But everyone you know is busy coming and going from Italy … and they're all bragging about what a wonderful time they had there. And for the rest of your life, you will say "Yes, that's where I was supposed to go. That's what I had planned."

And the pain of that will never, ever, ever, ever go away … because the loss of that dream is a very, very significant loss.

But … if you spend your life mourning the fact that you didn't get to Italy, you may never be free to enjoy the very special, the very lovely things … about Holland.

We are fully aware that despite being 5'4 and 125 lbs., Skyler may be our "little boy" forever. He could continue requiring assistance 24/7 for every task a grown man should be able to do for himself while we all grow old together. It has taken many years of deep thought and prayer, but I recently came to terms with the reality that Skyler will never drive a car, graduate high school or college, get married, have children, live on his own, or perhaps even utter a word. And that's honestly fine with me. Accepting that fate almost broke me but now I recognize God's blessing of choosing me and Josh to guide this gentle giant through life. Demonstrating true acceptance in my mind entails living for today and enjoying Skyler for all the joy he brings … while not wishing that he could do or be something more. I will always pursue the expertise of therapists and physicians to ensure Skyler is living his full potential, but if Skyler's abilities have reached their ceiling, I'm still a very proud momma.

It has taken many years of deep thought and prayer, but I recently came to terms with the reality that Skyler will never drive a car, graduate high school or college, get married, have children, live on his own, or perhaps even utter a word.

A Special Kind of Love

My love for Skyler knows no bounds and while autism presents various challenges for how he lives day to day, it does not define *who* Skyler is. A diagnosis is not a personality or a heart, nor is it a box in which my son is trapped. Being autistic does not devalue or diminish his contributions to this world. I love Skyler because he made me a mother for the first time. Although he can't verbalize the words "Mom" or "I love you," I know just by the way he looks at me and kisses me on the cheek each night before bed that he is aware of who I am and loves me, too. Skyler teaches me to be brave, strong and courageous. He's taught me that when I'm tired and feel like giving up, I can keep going. He's also taught me that there are other means of communication beyond speaking. He has taught me to look and listen and to trust my gut.

Skyler teaches me to be brave, strong and courageous. He's taught me that when I'm tired and feel like giving up, I can keep going.

I love Skyler for always being patient with me as I learn what he needs and work to understand his forms of communication.

I love Skyler for his view of the world and for seeing and hearing things most people probably do not.

I love Skyler for never holding back his emotions and for having the most amazing, deep belly laugh I've ever heard. Although it can be extremely frustrating for all of us to correctly identify his feelings of love, anger, happiness, pain and sadness, he never gives up trying to communicate with us.

I love Skyler and his love for *Sesame Street*, for nearly every kind of music, for Qdoba burrito bowls, bun-less cheeseburgers, macaroni and cheese, wrestling with Josh, and his ability to negotiate with only his eyes.

I love Skyler because he is true to himself and because every single day is the best day of his life.

I love Skyler because he works extremely hard to be part of a world that makes no sense to him and often misunderstands and judges him unfairly.

I love Skyler exactly how God made him and I hope that I love him exactly how he needs me to.

Having a child with autism hasn't made me a different parent, but perhaps it's made me a more purposeful one. Autism doesn't alter the way I love my son, nor does it force me to love him differently from how I love Kendall. Autism is a part of my family's journey, and it forever will be. A long time ago, I accepted that my family does not fit into that "ordinary" mold. We do what we can to get through every challenge and find the beauty in autism, and the beauty in our special family. It is our daily mission to ensure that autism does not stifle our dreams — mine, Josh's, Kendall's or Skyler's. We keep dreaming and striving and laughing and showing up every single day.

Our attempt at normalcy and happiness, as we define it, is not diminished. I'm proud of the family we have become — our tenacity and our silliness, our devotion to one another, and our "no excuses" approach to life. I'm proud of Kendall for her big heart and her maturity and her intuitive nature. I am proud of Josh for becoming a father and a special soul-mate to Skyler. I am proud of Skyler for being brave and dancing to the music, come what may.

As for me, I'm learning to be a willing and enthusiastic tour guide on this life's journey. As time has passed and autism families and experts have found one another, the road has become less lonely. But it's not always easy. I realize there will forever be countless battles to fight and ignorance about the disorder to overcome, but I'm up for the challenge. And, in the end, it's not about me. I'm not just a warrior mom; we are a warrior family.

As I look back, I knew my life had purpose before Skyler was born. But now I truly know what I've been put on this earth to do. I am the mother of two amazing children, one of whom happens to have autism. And I love them. I will never stop pushing both of my children to be their very best — cheering for them, advocating for them, supporting them and giving every ounce of my effort to ensure their safety, health and happiness. Skyler and Kendall are my purpose

This is my life. And it's beautiful beyond anything I could have ever dreamed.

My Life in Pictures

Epilogue

Like the old saying goes, *"When man plans, God laughs."* Never have truer words been demonstrated than during what our world is experiencing at the moment this book is being released.

After much writing, planning and editing, this memoir was gearing up to be marketed to the masses when the COVID-19 pandemic struck and forever changed daily lives throughout the world.
It's not unlike many of the tragedies from the past — we will always remember the year 2020 for the uncertainty and forced isolation the dreaded and deadly virus imposed on us all.

When the CDC and government officials began shutting down businesses, implementing personal safety precautions and issuing stay-at-home orders, I took them seriously. I was frightened by the knowledge that, by simply going to the grocery store, I could possibly bring the virus into my home where a child with a compromised immune system lives. I was honestly shocked at how many people turned a blind eye to the severity of the situation during the initial weeks (and again after summer arrived and people began giving into their "cabin fever") despite the saturation of media coverage and expert medical advice. Many of those who disregarded the order for social distancing argued that people can't be expected to implement such drastic measures without time to process and ease into it. Believe me, as an autism parent, the incredible irony of how frustrated people have gotten with last-minute schedule changes and the loneliness caused by being isolated from the general public is not lost on me. I wanted to shout my book title from the rooftop for all to hear: "Welcome to my life!"

Because that isolation and that sense that the world has shifted on its axis is essentially how most autistics and their family members feel every day. Heck, even the illustrated photos with step-by-step proper hand-washing techniques being shared by neurotypicals on social media a thousand times a day were clearly stolen straight out of our therapy handbooks!

Like most parents, the overwhelming and sudden burden of adding the title "full-time home-school teacher" to my countless other responsibilities made me a nervous wreck. While I was devastated for Kendall that her freshman year of high school ended so abruptly and without proper closure, I wasn't concerned with the online coursework that would be required to complete her school year. She has always been a straight-A student and thankfully didn't need any assistance from me (which was great, because I don't remember anything useful from biology or algebra II!). My biggest anxiety, of course, set in when thinking about Skyler's therapy and the closure of his ABA center.

As you've surely gathered from reading this book, most people with special needs thrive when maintaining a specific routine. Any deviation (from the schedule or regarding places they expect to visit or people they are used to seeing on a daily basis) generates quite a bit of chaos. So, when the dreaded text thread came out revealing that Skyler's ABA center would be closed for an undetermined period of time, the stability of my mental health took a massive hit. As with any major family crisis, Josh and I came together, cursed a little, prayed a little and agreed that we would figure out a plan.

We grabbed our calendars, both of which had a lot of cross through and eraser marks at this point, and penciled in how we would tag team entertaining Skyler around each of our daily, virtual work obligations. We put a lot of mileage on our cars by taking Skyler for lengthy drives around town and wore the tread off our shoes taking him for four or five stroller rides per day around the neighborhood. Heck, even our dog started hiding from us because she just couldn't handle any more walks!

Thankfully, that arrangement only lasted the first week. We were completely at our wits' end with the banging and destruction Skyler was causing (because he couldn't comprehend why we were making him stay home, forcing every day to feel like a LONG Saturday). By the grace of God, Skyler's BCBA (Board Certified Behavioral Analyst) — the expert who oversees all of Skyler's programming and therapists — reached out to us and asked if we would like to try in-home therapy with a few registered behavioral technicians (RBTs) who had the desire and availability to work with Skyler in the afternoons. We were elated! Although setting up a card table and chairs in his bedroom to create a makeshift classroom would likely present some issues, it was definitely worth a try.

Two straight weeks of in-home therapy, sadly, was not the answer. Skyler banged even harder on his bedroom walls and closet doors and threw every tool or toy his therapists tried to use with him, regardless of the breaks he was given every two minutes. My assumption, because he's unable to articulate his complaints, was that isolating him and turning the "safe place" where he relaxes after a hard day into a makeshift school room where he's required to complete work was not gonna fly. As much as we appreciated the thoughtfulness and compassion of the RBTs to overlook the possible health concerns (i.e., potential exposure to coronavirus) by entering our home, the benefit of keeping Skyler on his therapy schedule was not worth the risk, especially given that he seemed more annoyed than overjoyed to see them at our front door.

Week four of the stay-at-home order was again spent with Josh and me tag teaming one-on-one time with Skyler while coordinating quality time with Kendall and completing our work commitments as well. Kendall was equally as heartbroken to hear that Skyler would no longer have therapy each day because now she would have to share our time and attention. This sharing of time, of course, was teenage code for locking herself in her room. How is it that teenagers can go from ignoring you by retreating into their bedroom 24/7 (and only surfacing when needing to replenish calories) to suddenly needing hourly suggestions on how to rectify their boredom? I figured this was the perfect time to revisit teaching her household responsibilities like laundry, cooking, budgeting and cleaning. So, during Josh's Uber obligations to Skyler, Kendall and I would conduct her lessons in what I like to call Mom's Home Economics *non*-elective course. Guess who won't come to me claiming to be bored ever again? (Wow, I just sounded exactly like my mother!)

By this point, more details and specifics about the novel coronavirus emerged, which again raised our level of concern for Skyler's health and well-being. It's not that we were dismissing the seriousness of any family member in our household contracting the virus, it's just that Skyler's body had recently recovered from his negative experience with a biologic drug that blunted his immune response ... and he was due to start a different injectable biologic very soon. My mother's intuition incessantly crept into my every thought several days leading up to what would be his first dose of the new medicine, and Josh and I agreed it absolutely wasn't worth the risk. I easily justified the decision to defy physician orders by blaming the unknown of COVID-19, but honestly, we couldn't bear the thought of Skyler suffering through abscesses, infections and horrible side effects that would most likely ravage his poor body once again.

Many years ago, during my research into new, non-evasive treatment ideas for Skyler, I came across the concept of biomedical intervention. A few of the methods used by interventionists, such as the hyperbaric oxygen chamber and the gluten-free, casein-free diet, really intrigued me and were implemented into Skyler's daily regimen for several years — each producing no noticeable benefits. At that stage in our lives, brokenhearted and feeling duped with false promises, I forced myself to tuck away that research and abandoned the idea that Skyler's aggression and anxiety could be diminished by means other than prescription medications.

You'll recall that just prior to the pandemic (January 2020), we took a trip to New York to follow up with Skyler's gastroenterologist. At that time, my gut instinct (no pun intended) and mother's intuition gave me a one-two punch. I kept replaying the same thought on loop in my head, *"I'm just not convinced that Skyler's intestinal and digestion issues are exclusively to blame for his at-times-terrorizing behaviors and that the only fix is through heavy doses of pills and injections."* Immediately, as our plane taxied to the gate, I reached out to a friend whose opinion I've always valued and respected due to her medical training as a nurse practitioner and her personal experience with an autistic child a handful of years older than Skyler.

Well, low and behold, minutes into our conversation, the term biomedical intervention came up again but this time, with Skyler being older, I felt more mentally equipped to connect some dots with his behaviors, illnesses and vitamin deficiencies. My updated research tells me that biomedical intervention is based on the idea that environmental factors can overwhelm a genetically susceptible child and cause physical problems in body chemistry, the digestive tract and/or the immune system. The practitioners in this field point out that the majority of autistic children also have digestive tract problems. They encourage parents and caregivers to watch for picky eating habits or food cravings, diarrhea, constipation, abnormal stools, abdominal pain or bloating, reflux, thrush or food sensitivities. These are all indicators of underlying woes in the gut. After both reading and hearing that information, I felt like someone punched *me* in the gut (again, no pun intended). Armed with this knowledge, I now had a reinvigorated passion and revived mission to diminish Skyler's suffering with a brand-new strategy. I love to envision what our lives would be like if a handful of all-natural vitamins and supplements could heal his GI issues and simultaneously curb his incessant banging.

Wasting no time, I immediately began digging up everything I could on the subject and scheduled a consultation with an expert in the area, but her first opening wasn't until April — three long months away. What a blessing that delay turned out to be because our appointment coincided with the purposed initiation of the new biologic and the worldwide pandemic! (Insert God's eye roll that I, again, think I can out-plan Him.)

In preparation for our consultation, we had to send out for a genetic panel on Skyler, which was easily gathered with a cheek swab. The analysis revealed several significant deficiencies and impaired metabolic pathways, which could've been written in Greek because it made zero sense to me. I felt like I was staring at a map that revealed the secret code to understanding Skyler's mind and internal challenges; now all I could do was wait and pray for someone knowledgeable to decode it.

Our virtual appointment was highly educational and, if I'm being honest, was again completely over my head. Based on the interventionist's advice, we began tapering off a few prescribed behavioral medications and implemented a rich protocol of vitamins and supplements. At the time of writing this, Skyler has been on his new regimen for six weeks and his ABA center, which recently reopened, has reported that he has been the most compliant, hard-working and smiley young man that they've seen in months. I recognize that with every treatment, suggestion, medication, therapy, etc. I've ever tried, this could yield the same result — little to no benefit. However, knowing that I'm restoring his body with the essential vitamins and supplements he truly needs (instead of injecting him with a potentially harmful chemical) gives me hope. And our doctors are learning from our experiences too; Skyler's GI doctor was supportive of our decision not to try another biologic and he's asked us to keep him posted on how the supplements are working. The doctor is hoping to gather additional data about autistic kids' digestion issues through our trials and experiences, and we're thrilled that he's interested. As for me, I'm hopeful that Skyler's frustrations and digestive pain will lesson, — or better yet, disappear — to clear the path for his beautiful smile and true purpose in life to shine bright.

My intention for writing this book was certainly not to glorify our life and provide all kinds of wisdom and advice as if I've got it all figured out. Clearly, I do not. I decided to share our family's raw and real story with you because it just may be the catalyst to empower another family to find the good in the struggles ... it just may be what another family needs to make it through to another day. There will always be curve balls thrown at our presently challenging daily life, but my goal is to just get through them one minute at a time. Will there likely be cussing, crying, frustration and glances to the sky with the expectation that God will answer my question of "why me?" Absolutely! But it's what happens *after* the meltdown that matters most. Perhaps as you were reading, you discovered information that was completely new to you or it's possible you were nodding your head and relating to every single word, feeling seen and heard and a little less alone.

It's what happens after the meltdown that matters most.

We each have a story and each of our stories matter. In fact, each of our stories is as unique as our own fingerprints ... our own DNA ... our own life's tapestry. Some of us openly share our stories, realizing that in sharing we are connecting. Others of us hide behind them, hoping that the real story never breaks through the story that we tell others and the story that we tell ourselves. Let's not hide. Let's welcome each other into our respective lives. Possibly, our stories are meant to be interwoven and, *together*, we can help change the lives of others ... maybe, even in the thick of the difficult times, we can find new ways to help others smile.

My smile helps me cope, but it also helps me refocus. It's how I navigate working full-time after sleepless nights with Skyler banging on the walls. It's how I find my normalcy in the midst of a daily life that I now realize isn't a part of everyone else's "normal." It's how I see the good in our lives even when our lives feel upside down. My smile — along with my silly and irreverent humor — helps me LIVE! And it helps my family live too.

It is my hope that you and *your* family are healthy, safe and smiling.

Josh, Skyler, Laurie and Kendall, 2015

Acknowledgments

First and foremost, I am grateful to my courageous son **Skyler** for constantly demonstrating that his diagnosis of autism does not equate to being broken or incapable of creating a tremendous impact on the world throughout his lifetime. He has *already* changed the world.

People routinely tell me what a blessing **my husband Josh** has been to our family and I know that God placed that incredible man in my life exactly when I needed him. No words can properly express my gratitude for his eagerness to jump right in and co-pilot this autism journey with me. He has been unwavering in his faith and constantly encouraged me as I worked hard to restore mine. Equally as important, he listens to all my crazy ideas, loves with every fiber of his being and is an excellent role model to our children. Josh, you are my rock, my comedic equal and best friend.

To my beautiful daughter, **Kendall**, who is wise beyond her years. Your gift of sarcasm and quick wit rivals my own but it's balanced by your enormous heart and thoughtfulness of every living thing on this planet. You are the strongest person I've ever known and I appreciate your patience and understanding when, admittedly, I don't have all the answers. God has huge plans for your future and I can't wait to brag about my daughter, the world's best veterinarian.

Having amazing support and relatability from close friends makes the unbearable easier to laugh through and it makes recovery time much faster — it's usually nothing a glass of wine can't fix! Shortly after moving to Southern Indiana, I met my dear friend **Monica Bottorff**, who is also Skyler's incredible Godmother and, lucky for me, she invited me to join a Bunco group comprising the most thoughtful and inspiring women in my community. Through our many shared experiences with our special-needs children, we've laughed, cried, complained and cheered for one another. I feel extremely blessed to call you amazing ladies my dear friends. I hope you all know how much I love and respect you.

The content for this book was drafted over and over in my mind for several years, but I held back on pursuing my dream of being an author for fear that my story was not unique enough to be shared. I owe a huge debt of gratitude to my friend and professional coach, **Laura Leaton of Anchored Elements Coaching and Training**, for her endless support, for the encouragement to be a trailblazer and for helping me recognize the importance of following the breadcrumbs while living in a constant state of being.

The writing process can be overwhelming and scary, but working with a knowledgeable and supportive book coach like **Cathy Fyock** made for a smooth and exciting journey. I thank you, Cathy, for all the education along the way and for the introduction to many members of my phenomenal publishing team!

One of the most impactful moments throughout my mission to become an author was meeting **Stephanie Feger**. Our instant bond has transitioned into an extraordinary friendship and led me to work with the best publishing company in the business! I'm forever indebted to **Kate Colbert**, owner of **Silver Tree Publishing**, who provided immeasurable value through meticulous copy editing, countless hours of putting out fires when the coronavirus pandemic threatened to ruin our launch schedule, and unwavering support every single step of the way; **Penny Tate,** who kept everything running smoothly behind the scenes and managed the deadlines that kept me on my toes; **Courtney Hudson Fox** for creating my gorgeous cover and overall book design; and of course Stephanie for the immense amount of time she spent on marketing, promotion and so many other important tasks to help make me and my story shine brightly.

During the early stages of my work, I was fortunate to enlist the kindness of friends and family, each of whom enthusiastically agreed to review, edit and provide feedback on my first manuscript draft. Most notably, my sister, **Beth Rayner**, went above and beyond when adding her own personal connection with Skyler to the heart of my story and used her plentiful years of experience grading student essays to ensure my memoir was free from errors.

My exceptional book launch team, which was over 70 members strong, has been a game changer throughout this process! To say I couldn't have done this without your assistance would be a huge understatement. I have been ecstatic to see the vast amount of publicity and shared connections you've generated on my behalf over a few short months. Taking the time out of your own busy lives to help promote my story has meant so much to me and I appreciate each one of you more than I can ever express.

I am so grateful to the amazing men and women who wrote endorsements for my book: **Angie Abbott, Kate Colbert, Emily Corum, Malinda Dalton-Cook, Kelly Davis, Rebecca Duvall Scott, Stephanie Feger, Cathy Fyock, Tom Harris, John Hackworth, Cliff Kresge, Arthur Krigsman, Laura Leaton, Jeff Mathe, Noopur Patel Ritter, Emily Perl Kingsley, Janet Pope, Beth Rayner, Ron Sandison, Samantha Setty, Penny Tate, Jerry Turning** and **Teresa Unnerstall**.

A special thank you to **Emily Perl Kingsley** for allowing me to reprint her powerful "Welcome to Holland" in this book, where it could touch more hearts.

I would be remiss to omit my gratitude for the following people who have had a tremendous impact on our family: **Kevin Lewis, restaurant manager of our New Albany, IN, Qdoba** store who has extended an insane amount of kindness and patience for the chaos our banging boy can bring into the restaurant; **Kristy Fox, my remarkable attorney** who I bonded with instantly for always understanding that I will never settle for less where my kids are concerned; **Joy Knopfmeier** who has offered calmness to our craziness and stress; **Beau and Lindsey Kerley, owners of Tucker's American Favorites restaurant in New Albany, IN,** and their many amazing servers for always greeting Skyler like Norm from *Cheers* and making him smile at the sight of his perfect bun-less cheeseburger and mashed potatoes just the way he likes it.

Thank you also to my talented friend **Anna May** of Anna May Photography for her gorgeous, professional family photos used throughout the book and on the front cover. Working with my family is extremely challenging and she always remains cool, calm and collected to ultimately capture the perfect shots. Equally as amazing behind the camera, **Brook Hollis** captured the professional headshots and marketing photos utilized for this book launch. Brook's infectious laughter and creativity made our day together a complete blast. Sincerest gratitude and appreciation to my friend, **Paul Loheide ("Doc")** for assuming the role of matchmaker and introducing me to my beloved husband Josh.

I have gained insight and perspective about Skyler's ever-changing needs from many of the caring professionals who have given helpful advice and/or contributed to his various treatment algorithms over the years, among them: **Dr. Timothy Corba, Dr. Arthur Krigsman,**

Carrie Schanie, NP, Dr. Stacy Trinkle, First Steps of Indiana, Lauren Elliott-Schweitzer, Adapt for Life Indiana, Bluegrass Center for Autism and Jenna Seewer with IPMG. Navigating through autism is extremely difficult and often leads to more questions than answers, but having incredible support from these individuals and organizations armed me with a renewed sense of purpose and energy.

Go Beyond the Book

and keep in Touch with Laurie L. Hellmann

Laurie L. Hellmann is a storyteller in every way! In addition to hosting a podcast for several years and being complimented for her conversational style that makes guests extremely comfortable, Laurie's messages, experiences and insights have been called inspirational and powerful. She openly shares her honest, personal journey from childhood to parenthood, and provides an educational component while igniting hope in others. Most of all, she is relatable and helps each person feel seen. Laurie believes that when we invite others to better understand the paths we are walking, we are better able to join hands and walk together with purpose.

Through her compassion, humor and desire to educate the world on the importance of personal growth and living your best life, Laurie motivates audiences to gain a renewed perspective and take action.

Hire Laurie to:

- Inspire your team, organization or audience with storytelling.

- Deliver a powerful and motivational keynote address to audiences of all sizes on topics including perspective, resiliency, inclusion, mental health and belief in a higher purpose.

- Facilitate workshops and lead panel discussions.

- Read from her book and host book signings.

Keep in Touch!

Listen to the Podcast on Apple, Spotify, YouTube Music or Audible:

Living the Sky Life ... Our Autism Journey

Send Laurie an email at:

Laurie@LaurieHellmann.com

For information on hiring Laurie, visit her website:

LaurieHellmann.com

Find, follow and share on social media:

LinkedIn.com/in/Laurie-Hellmann-1a2ba410/

Facebook.com/WelcomeToMyAutismLife

Instagram.com/WelcomeToMyLife_LaurieHellmann

Welcome to My Life: A Personal Parenting Journey Through Autism is Book #1 in the "Purposeful Journey" series. Book #2, *Selling Vegetables to Drunks,* is available everywhere books are sold.

You, Too, Can Generate Inclusion and Acceptance

Reach out to parents and caregivers in your community who may be struggling. Offer assistance or speak up on their behalf if someone is lacking compassion or understanding for their situation.

Share your story somehow or somewhere (perhaps as a guest on my podcast). The world needs your contribution and the "village" of support is eagerly waiting to embrace you.

Allow yourself to view the world and *all* its people with renewed perspective. Now that you know how severe one end of the autism spectrum can be, please don't dismiss a family's pain for an "unruly child who needs better discipline."

Pray for an inclusive world, where everyone has something important to say, regardless of their means for communicating it.

About the Author

Laurie L. Hellmann is
originally from Marshall,
Michigan, and moved to
Southern Indiana following
graduation from Ball State
University in 1997 with
a Bachelor of Science degree
in Legal Administration. She
went on to earn a Master
of Business Administration

degree from Indiana University Southeast. When her first child,
Skyler, was diagnosed with autism in 2006 at the age of three, Laurie
immediately began exploring treatment options and found that the
medical community still knew very little about the cause, treatment
and prognosis of this puzzling disorder. Laurie has spent the past 14
years fiercely navigating through therapies, medications and countless other medical and personal challenges with her son, all while
continuing to fight and be the voice for other families with a loved
one on the autism spectrum.

Laurie and her husband, Josh, are both distance runners, having each
completed 10 full marathons. Running is what brought them together
and continues to be an important shared passion. With the focus
on autism awareness and fundraising, Laurie has raised close to
$10,000 through her races for local autism programs. When she's not
advocating for her son, Laurie has enjoyed being a dance mom and
supporting her daughter Kendall's competitive dance team from

2017-2020 and looks forward to their next mother/daughter bonding adventures.

Professionally, Laurie has more than 20 years of experience in sales and leadership. She speaks to audiences of all sizes on topics including perspective, resiliency, self-advocacy and belief in a higher purpose. She is the host of the podcast "Living the Sky Life — Our Autism Journey." *Welcome to My Life* is Laurie's first book.

Bonus Chapter

Selling Vegetables to Drunks
by Laurie L. Hellmann

Here we go again — commemorating another book and another chance to meet you, my reader, in a truly honest, raw, vulnerable and complete way. Thank you for this opportunity — for being here with me when it's scary. I am ready (finally!) and I hope you are ready too. I entitled my first book *Welcome to My Life* and, right now, in this second book, I'd like to welcome you to my family. In the pages that follow, you'll meet them all: my mother and father, my sister, aunts and uncles, two husbands (for worse and for better), and my two spectacular children, Skyler and Kendall. While my parenting journey has been periodically bumpy — often requiring that I navigate uncharted, unrelatable terrain — I have come to understand that my own transition from being someone's child to being some children's mother has taken me on a purposeful journey to who I was meant to be. Motherhood is the teaching tool that has guided (and healed) my life; being a mom (sometimes under overwhelming circumstances) has offered me the chance to take on the most important role I didn't realize I needed. It is a role and an opportunity that God had prepared me for all along.

As you are about to learn, my childhood wasn't all popsicles and bedtime stories. It was rough, complicated and painful. It forced me to grow up too fast, to confront big emotions like fear and shame, and to craft an adult life that simultaneously ran far, far away from where I'd been while never quite being able to escape where I had been. I've had career success and personal growth, but none of it helped me heal from my own childhood. It was the miraculous journey of becoming a mother — and slaying my own demons in service to my children — that has presented me with the opportunity to rewrite my story, using all that I'd learned (the hard way) as fuel to provide my children with the safe, loving childhood that was withheld from me. I always promised myself that no matter what my motherhood journey brought with it, I would break the cycle of abuse and addiction that had plagued my family for generations. It would end with me. Banned from my home would be the harsh words and stinging criticisms that leave wounds of self-doubt and internal suffering not easily or quickly healed. Those words, those looks, those behaviors, those raised voices and raised eyebrows — they can brand us emotionally to a depth that controls your every thought, action and opinion through the entirety of your life ... unless you're willing to acknowledge it and work to release it. *I would do better*, I promised myself and my children. The kinds of rage and impatience that characterized my youth would be replaced with the emotional and physical connection that was significantly lacking throughout my childhood. I was going to give my children everything I had needed and not received. I was not going to "live vicariously" through them, as far too many parents do, but I was going to *heal* through them as they were nurtured into their best selves, safe to be whoever they were destined to be.

I was committed to showing up differently as a parent — to giving my kids the childhood of my dashed and deferred dreams and to providing them with the kind of formative years they wouldn't have to seek therapy to recover from.

All parents, despite their best efforts, pass on both good and unde-
sirable traits to their children. But some parents fall far, far short on
exhibiting "best efforts." Some show up, just barely, to this odyssey
we call "parenthood." I was raised in a home with addiction at the
forefront. My sister, my mom and I were too busy swimming in
alcohol and cruelty — just trying to keep our heads above water from
day to day as the children and spouse of one of the town drunks — to
get any positive takeaways from family life. Looking back, I don't see
the "lessons," "values" or even traditions that I hear other people talk
about when it comes to their upbringings; I just see an overpowering
spotlight on the negatives, such as low self-esteem, the practice of
denial, poor anger management skills, poor emotional regulation
skills, narcissism, passive-aggressive behavior, and possibly the
genetic markers for addiction and depression. My childhood was
a dark time and, until very recently, I didn't want to talk about it.
And to be fair, while both my parents were alive, I didn't feel I *could*
talk about it.

We each have a story, and each of our stories matters. But does mine
matter *enough* to rock the boat of my immediate and extended family
to finally tell the truth — confidently, publicly and without shame ...
here, in a book for you? I think it does. So, after years of excuses as to
why I should wait to write and publish this memoir, here we are.

I've paused and resumed the drafting of this book many times until
my reasons to complete it finally outweighed my reasons to refrain.
Sometimes while writing and revisiting the painful events throughout
my childhood — moments that I thought had been fully dissected
and resolved during years of therapy — I was overcome with an unex-
pected emotional response. The tears streaming down my face as
I typed each disturbing memory in grave detail indicated that those
buried feelings and insecurities were alive and well and that I needed
to release them to officially move on and enjoy my life.

I have heard the expression "We are only as sick as our secrets," and that struck a chord with me. We all — even those with relatively idyllic childhoods and lives full of fortune and blessings — harbor some sort of secret that we have kept (often for years or decades) out of shame or obligation or fear. I've been keeping secrets my whole life. I was distracted with fear and worry that sharing my story at the wrong time could be damaging to others. I kept telling myself that "once enough time passed" or when the main offender in most of my stories was no longer around ("after my dad dies"), sharing my truth would be easier. I don't know that I'd say it's "easier," but I do feel like it's time. I realize that as I prepare to tell you my story — a story that belongs to many members of my family but that is still very much mine to tell — the words I'm about to say cannot be rescinded. The burden of hurting others through what I reveal to those on the periphery of our family remains a heavy weight on my shoulders.

In the end, there is no such thing as "perfect timing" — only "I feel ready." Through the process of writing and editing this book, I have gained immeasurable clarity and confidence about who I am as an individual, a wife, a sister, a daughter, a friend and a mother. Parenting Skyler and Kendall, while simultaneously acknowledging the little girl inside me, has helped me make sense of my childhood and release myself from the negative labels and insecurities that have haunted me my entire life. I am no longer envious of people who have had "easy" childhoods, but instead consider myself stronger and wiser for having overcome mine. I've been offered the opportunity to view the world differently — a world in which God gives you what you *need* instead of what you *want*, as a means of illuminating your ultimate purpose.

In sharing the story of my life, I wish to validate the young child in all of us who may still suffer from low self-esteem or the belief that they can't achieve incredible things because someone in their life programmed them to believe that to be true. More importantly,

I want that inner child to understand one of the biggest lessons I've learned: feelings aren't facts. My parenting philosophy is all about feelings, but not the kind of feelings that nearly destroyed me when I was growing up. My primary focus while raising both of my children has been ensuring that I provide them with the basic emotional foundation they deserve from me — validation, affection and acceptance — while empowering them to live with confidence, never having to feel a single negative thing about themselves. "You worthless piece of ..." are words that were said to me but never said to my children. It is my deepest hope that my children feel only positive things about themselves and that the only feelings I "give" them are ones that make them feel worthy, loved, respected and accepted for precisely who they are.

In every chapter of this book, I endeavor to be transparent and raw, and I refuse to let fear and resentment continue to take up precious real estate in my mind. As you are reading, I hope my work (and the risks I take) in this regard will inspire you to break free of whatever may be holding *you* back from living *your* best life. I believe that our life experiences are always teaching us something — and preparing us for or connecting us to what is yet to come. But it takes a shift in perspective and a big dose of courage to see the true beauty of where we've been or the purposeful life lessons that are borne from our challenges.

www.ingramcontent.com/pod-product-compliance
Lightning Source LLC
Chambersburg PA
CBHW070659130626

46553CB00005B/1764